LE CORBUSIER

BY PETER BLAKE

PELICAN BOOK A605

LE CORBUSIER
ARCHITECTURE AND FORM
BY PETER BLAKE

PENGUIN BOOKS

Penguin Books Inc., 3300 Clipper Mill Road, Baltimore, Maryland

The Master Builders was originally published by Alfred A. Knopf Inc. This Pelican edition, taken from *The Master Builders,* first published 1964 by arrangement with Alfred A. Knopf Inc.

Printed in the United States of America

FOR CHRISTINA, CASEY, KATHY, BILLY, AND ELIZABETH

ACKNOWLEDGEMENTS

I am indebted in particular to the complete record of Le Corbusier's work published over the years by the Swiss architect Willy Boesiger, and, of course, to the many published pronouncements on his work by Le Corbusier himself. It goes without saying that he had no direct or indirect part in the preparation of this book; indeed, I have met M. Le Corbusier only a few times over the past twenty years or so, and know him only very casually. However, I found his buildings, many of which I have seen, quite eloquent enough.

I am further indebted to my friend Philip C. Johnson (and to many of my other architect-friends) for their frequent, stimulating, irreverent, and penetrating comments on the present architectural scene; to Walter McQuade, Henry Robbins, and Ivan von Auw for reading this manuscript and offering valuable suggestions; and to innumerable others who have supplied me with factual details that I would, otherwise, have found inaccessible. None of these friends is in any way responsible for the value judgements or opinions expressed by me.

PETER BLAKE
New York, 1963

PREFACE

At no time in the recorded history of architecture has the manner in which men build undergone changes as radical as those that have occurred during the past century. Under the pressure of the tremendous growth in the earth's population, new developments took place in almost every field of human endeavour; but these developments were nowhere more spectacular than in the field of architecture.

Because more and more people had to be housed and employed in large urban centres, builders had to learn to build vertically. Technology provided two essential tools: the steel-framed building that could rise to great heights without requiring enormously thick walls at ground level; and the mechanical elevator. Because more and more goods had to be manufactured by mass-production methods on large assembly lines, builders had to learn to roof over very large spaces with uninterrupted spans, and technology again produced the answers in terms of great iron-and-glass halls and later in terms of large, reinforced-concrete vaults. And because transportation and communication became essential tools without which a mass society could not hope to function properly, builders had to learn to construct great bridges and viaducts, great railroad sheds, canals, and harbours.

Indeed, most of the building types that are now a part of our daily lives did not even exist before 1850. The modern factory, the modern skyscraper, the shopping centre, the modern school, and the modern hospital – all these are completely new inventions, with almost no antecedents prior to the middle of the nineteenth century. When architects first developed some of these new building types, they had a very hard time finding the right 'style' for these new-fangled structures. For the nineteenth century was entirely eclectic, and every respectable building (most architects thought) had to follow stylistic precedent – whether medieval-romantic, or renaissance-classical.

But where in the Middle Ages or in the Renaissance was there a precedent for a skyscraper? Where was there a precedent for a steel mill or a railroad shed? Some architects evaded the issue by deciding, quite simply, that these new building types belonged in the realm of engineering rather than polite architecture. Others tried to stretch the eclectic patterns to fit the new façades – and failed. And there were a few – a very few – who faced the new problems squarely and saw in them a great challenge to their creative abilities. These few architects and engineers displayed an inventiveness unmatched in any other period of building: within the span of a single generation, this handful of pioneers in effect created an entirely new vocabulary of building types, and gave each of these building types a distinctive and expressive face of its own.

These early pioneers are now a part of architectural history: Louis Sullivan, the architect who, almost single-handed, turned the skyscraper into architecture; Joseph Paxton, the landscape-designer who built the London Crystal Palace in 1851 – an exhibition hall covering some eighteen acres of ground, and made almost entirely of prefabricated iron and glass elements; and others before and after him, in England, Germany, and the United States, men who created the first great structures using the materials of the Industrial Revolution. And, finally, the theorists and practitioners who, in metal, glass, concrete, and stone, reasserted certain qualities of unaffected structure and unadorned form. All of them laid the foundations for what we know today as modern architecture.

Yet, regardless of the spirit of the times, regardless of the daring of engineers and the vision of those architects who broke with the past, modern architecture could not have gone far beyond purely utilitarian solutions without the appearance, around the turn of the century and in the decade following it, of half a dozen great individual artists who knew, instinctively, what they must do with the new tools at hand.

This is the first in a series of three monographs, each of which deals with the life and work of one member of this small group. The present volume tells the story of Charles-Édouard Jeanneret, better known as Le Corbusier, native of Switzerland and a citizen of France. The second volume deals with Ludwig Mies van der Rohe, native of the German Rhineland and now a citizen of the United States. And the third is concerned with the life and work of Frank Lloyd Wright, an American largely of Welsh ancestry.

These three men did not do it alone; indeed, there were others who may have contributed a great deal more in certain areas of modern architecture: Walter Gropius certainly did more towards the establishment of a modern *rationale* – in architectural education, in the industrialization of building, and in the analysis of social problems – than any of these three masters; Eric Mendelsohn, Alvar Aalto, Richard Neutra, and others produced many solutions of a much more practical nature than the three men we have singled out; and there were engineers like Robert Maillart, Eugène Freyssinet, and Pier Luigi Nervi who understood much better than these three men the potentialities of all the new structural techniques which the masters discussed so airily and sometimes experimented with so primitively.

Still, Le Corbusier, Mies van der Rohe, and Wright will ultimately appear more important than their contemporaries because they were greater as artists – as poets of architecture. Scientists, engineers, and businessmen are essential to the creation of a civilization; but it always takes poets to point the way. 'A map of the world that does not include Utopia is not worth even glancing at,' Oscar Wilde once said. The poets, not the practical men, are the ones who put Utopia on that map.

Of the three poets, of the three master builders we have singled out, Le Corbusier is the most sophisticated, the most civilized, and the most prolific. Being French by detoured origin, he is the heir to the finest traditions of the Western world, and this fact has had an extraordinarily liberating effect both upon his personality and upon the quality of his work. In the lives of Mies van der Rohe and Wright, concepts such as 'discipline' and 'puritanism', respectively, play an important and often an inhibiting part. But Le Corbusier's ancestors have been exceedingly well disciplined and moral for so very long that such straightjackets were discarded generations ago. To Le Corbusier, as to all heirs to the traditions of the Mediterranean, humanity's greatest achievement is the rule of law – in politics, as well as in art; and to him, also, the sole purpose of the rule of law is to make men free to act heroically, whether as statesmen, as poets, or as artists. Mies van der Rohe is haunted by the spectre of a disorderly world; Wright was a very self-conscious rebel against puritanism; but to Le Corbusier these issues never appeared important – they were settled long ago.

Le Corbusier has often been compared with Leonardo and Michelangelo. These comparisons are not presumptuous, as we hope to show. But they are surprising in another sense. For the age of Leonardo and of Michelangelo was an age of few men, living in small societies governed by a very few rich and powerful princes and patrons. In such an age, a great artist willing to submit to the general equation of power and wealth could have had little trouble making his mark.

But Le Corbusier's world is very different: a world of terrifying population growth, a world whose rulers judge most success in economic terms. In architecture this can be an insurmountable obstacle: to build, nowadays, one must have a client willing to risk a considerable investment – whereas to paint, to sculpt, to compose music, or to write a poem, one needs only oneself. To be an architectural innovator in a time like this is to overcome enormous practical difficulties – for no businessman and no governmental authority wishes to risk great sums to prove the theories of some *avant-garde* dreamer.

Yet, in spite of these formidable obstacles, Le Corbusier not only drew and painted and wrote, but built as well. And how well! Labouring under economic pressures that would have felled a Phidias or a Brunelleschi, Le Corbusier produced architecture of such power – and often out of virtually nothing – that the world of building will never again be the same. For although many of his most forceful buildings were made not out of marble, bronze, crystal, or mosaics, but only out of sand and cement and gravel, they did possess the one ingredient that has, in the end, shaped the architecture of every significant civilization. That ingredient is passion. Even the ruins of some of Le Corbusier's earliest, abandoned villas possess that single, most important ingredient. And, because they do, they will live even when the cement has turned to dust.

When the late abstract painter Fernand Léger first met Le Corbusier in 1921, the occasion turned out to be something to remember. Léger was standing on the terrace of the Rotonde, in Montparnasse, when a friend said to him: 'Just wait, you are about to see a very odd specimen. He goes bicycling in a derby hat.' A few minutes later, Léger recalled, there was a strange apparition, a creature, very stiff, completely in silhouette, 'an extraordinarily mobile object under a derby hat, with spectacles and wearing a dark suit'. To Léger, this creature looked more like a clergyman or, better still, like an English clergyman, than a visionary pamphleteer on architecture, painting, and the world in general. 'He advanced quietly,' Léger said, 'scrupulously obeying the laws of perspective.'

Charles-Édouard Jeanneret – the 'extraordinarily mobile object under the derby hat' – was born on 6 October 1887 in the small watch-making town of La Chaux-de-Fonds, near Neuchâtel, in Switzerland. His family, like just about everyone else in the town, had been connected for generations with the manufacture of watches; both his father and mother were professional engravers of watch cases. By ancestry Jeanneret is French; some of his forebears were Albigensians – fanatical French heretics of the fourteenth century who fled into the Alps to escape persecution in their homeland. Most of them were peasants, and their harsh fate made them reserved, cold, and suspicious of the world around them. One of Jeanneret's southern French ancestors was called Le Corbusier, and he assumed that name in 1923 to distinguish between two of his multiple personalities – those of painter and of architect.

Le Corbusier has not been known to wear a derby hat in quite some time, yet his appearance is almost as baffling as it must have been in the twenties. His face has the flat, almost monumental cast of an Easter Island head. It looks dead white, much whiter than it really is, because Le Corbusier has, for many years, worn the blackest, most exactly circular, and thickest-edged horn-rimmed glasses known to the optical trade. These glasses, his personal emblem, appear in photographs of his early houses, casually left lying on a kitchen table or a mantelpiece. Together with the razor-edged features of his face, the black-rimmed spectacles soon brought Le Corbusier the nickname of 'Corbu' – a variation on the word *corbeau*, or 'raven'. He is now known as Corbu among architects all over the world. (In recent years, some of them have donned similar black-edged glasses, presumably to show their solidarity with Corbu. As a result, a typical meeting of the *avant-garde* nowadays tends to look like a convocation of owls, ravens, or giant pandas – depending upon the avant-gardist's other physical characteristics.)

Although Corbu has many admirers, he has very few close friends; for the personality he presents to much of the outside world is almost a caricature of all the ancestral and geographical influences one might expect to have shaped him. On casual acquaintance he appears cold, suspicious, pugnacious, sarcastic (but quite humourless about himself), and arrogant. Most of his admirers have learned to put up with this rather unappealing image, explaining it by referring to the bitter fight for recognition which Le Corbusier has had to wage most of his life. But, to the few people who know him well, Corbu is an entirely different sort of person: a man of tremendous charm, wit, and great warmth; of scholarship, vision, and superb taste. All these qualities are evident in his work and in his extensive writings. Yet, because the world, to him, seems almost always to have been populated with real or, at least, potential enemies, Corbu wears the mask of a suspicious Swiss peasant, or, worse still, of a suspicious Swiss *petit-bourgeois*.

Under these circumstances, it is not surprising that Corbu evokes only extreme responses in those who have worked with him. Some of the architects who were associated with him on the initial planning of the United Nations Headquarters in New York have said, more or less publicly, that they would never again touch a project in which Le Corbusier had any part. On the other hand, Oscar Niemeyer, the brilliant young Brazilian architect who played a major role in that same collaborative effort, will state without the slightest hesitation that he considers Le Corbusier the Leonardo da Vinci of our epoch, and that Corbu deserves all the respect, honour, and affection due to an artist of such calibre. Many of Corbu's contemporaries in architecture agree. Walter Gropius, the most important educator and theoretician

of the modern movement, who first met Le Corbusier in 1910, has said that it will take an entire generation of architects to realize all the visionary concepts Corbu has outlined in his innumerable sketches and projects. And Mies van der Rohe, an architect whom many consider on a par with Le Corbusier, recalled recently that when he was Director of the famous Weissenhof development in Stuttgart, in 1927 – a full-scale architectural exhibition in which most of the leading modernists of the day contributed one or two important buildings – he started out by inviting Corbu and giving him first choice of a site for his buildings. 'Naturally, he picked the best one,' Mies van der Rohe commented with a grin. 'He has quite an eye! And I would give him first choice again under similar circumstances, any time!'

Corbu's extraordinary talent and his insatiable capacity for absorbing visual experiences everywhere and in all periods of art became evident at a very early age. When he was only fourteen years old he qualified for the École d'Art at La Chaux-de-Fonds, a kind of technical high school set up for the express purpose of training engravers for the watchmaking industries in the town. There he became the student of Professor L'Éplattenier. Several years later Corbu described L'Éplattenier as 'a fascinating teacher . . . a master who opened to me the gateways to the world of art. With him, we lost ourselves in the art of all ages and of all lands.' L'Éplattenier encouraged his young student to concentrate on architecture, as well as to participate in the work of a newly formed department for sculpture and for mural painting.

The Art School in his home town became a major influence in Corbu's life throughout his younger years – in fact until he moved to Paris for good at the age of thirty. As its most promising student, Corbu was commissioned, when he was only eighteen, to design and build a villa for one of the Art School's trustees. Although this first building is not considered particularly significant in the light of his later work, it did enable Corbu to take the first of a series of major trips that carried him beyond the borders of Switzerland – trips that proved to be of considerable importance in his future development. The year was 1906, and Corbu spent much of it in Italy and Austria. Italy was his first introduction to the plasticity of white stucco forms in the bright sun, seen against a Mediterranean sky. Austria was his first introduction to the Art Nouveau movement in general, and to the architect Josef Hoffmann in particular.

Art Nouveau was a short-lived but enormously important movement, world-wide in scope. It had its protagonists in England, Germany, France, Belgium, Spain, the United States, and elsewhere. In the history of art there are occasional movements whose actual output is highly questionable, but whose impact upon what went on before them (and what was to come later) is tremendous. Art Nouveau was such a movement; it began as a protest against nineteenth-century eclecticism – neo-classicism in particular – and it ended by destroying not only eclecticism, but itself as well. It attempted to substitute a new kind of honesty in design for the sham of classical imitation, and it looked for this new kind of honesty in forms that could be found in nature – in trees, flowers, swirling clouds, and craggy rocks. For a rather short period – thirty or forty years – Art Nouveau dominated all forms of creative expression, from the poster art of Toulouse-Lautrec to the furniture of Guimard. Before long, however, its influence began to pall: the premise upon which it had been based (that forms in nature were more valid sources of inspiration than forms in the Renaissance or in the Gothic) seemed to collapse; yet the movement did not fade away until it had completely destroyed both neo-classicism and the Gothic Revival as serious, creative points of view. And when Art Nouveau finally died, it had opened the gates to something Corbu was to call, in later years, the New Vision – the style of a new industrial epoch.

Joseph Hoffman's Wiener Werkstätte (Viennese Workshops) were a highly sophisticated offspring of the Art Nouveau movement. Unlike Art Nouveau designers such as Louis Tiffany in the United States, who found 'honesty' in the tulip form and turned it into a vase, Hoffmann never quite succumbed to the purely decorative aspects of the Art Nouveau – the 'enervating atmosphere' of the movement, as the art historian Nikolaus Pevsner calls it. Certainly Hoffmann, being Viennese, was playful; but he was also 'modern' in the sense that he looked for inspiration in things that were characteristic of the time in which he lived, such as the forms of machines. Corbu worked for Hoffmann very briefly in 1908; but when the latter suggested a more permanent arrangement, Corbu made his excuses. Although he was still in his early twenties, it was clear to him that the fondness for decorative panels in the Art Nouveau manner, which characterized most of Hoffmann's work, was not for him. Still, he had seen the outlines of a new and exciting discipline beyond Hoffmann's playful details, and he appreciated this underlying discipline while rejecting the surface décor.

Here, perhaps, is the first important manifestation of a quality that sets Le Corbusier apart from most of his contemporaries. That quality is his faultless taste. Frank Lloyd Wright, whose fundamental contributions to architecture may someday be considered more important than those of Le Corbusier, possessed the taste of a Victorian embroiderer. His sense of colour, of decoration, often even of form was, to put it mildly, disconcerting. Mies van der Rohe's taste is as impeccable as a fine Savile Row suit, yet it is so perfect for precisely the same reason that a fine Savile Row suit is perfect: because Mies, as he is generally referred to, takes no chances. But Corbu not only takes a new chance with every new building; he also manages, generally, to win his gamble. Even the outrageously 'primitive' architecture he began to produce after the Second World War – at a time when everyone expected him to lead the way towards a new world of luminous plastics and shining metal – even this 'new brutalism' (as an English magazine called it) had a splendour, an absence of grossness combined with sheer guts, in short, a perfection of taste which no one, not even Corbu's many imitators, was able to copy.

So, when he saw Hoffmann's doilies stuck on Machine Art buildings, Corbu politely said no. Yet he did see the Machine Art – as, indeed, he saw everything else around him. On every trip he was to take, on every visit to a new Greek Island or a new American metropolis, Le Corbusier would store away impressions, ideas, forms, colours that might not turn up again in his work for decades to come. He generally carried his sketchbooks with him, filling them with quick, dramatic, incisive drawings of a casual object here or a whole city there. These sketches in themselves reveal more about Le Corbusier's clear vision than the thousands of words he has put on paper. They reveal, above all, that he is not primarily a technician or a social philosopher or a city planner – as his books sometimes make him appear – but a plastic artist of supreme authority.

T W O

In 1908 Le Corbusier went to Paris for his first extended visit. Although he was only twenty years old, he knew precisely what he was looking for: like the adherents of Art Nouveau, he was looking for a new kind of honesty; but, unlike them, he was looking for it in the geometry of the machine forms that seemed to typify his time.

No artist, however creative, can avoid being influenced by the spirit of his time; Le Corbusier has not only been influenced, he has consistently pictured himself as a sort of spokesman for that spirit. To re-create, for a moment, the spirit of Paris in 1908, it is important to recall a number of significant events: the year before, Picasso had painted his *Les Demoiselles d'Avignon*, 'the first Cubist picture', according to Alfred Barr. The naturalism of Picasso's earlier work had been replaced by a painting resolved into flat, geometric elements. Braque, too, was painting his first Cubist pictures; his *Houses at l'Estaque*, done in 1908, was a composition of cubes and pyramids, very precisely rendered. Meanwhile, Cézanne's rather questionable assertion that 'everything in nature is formed according to the sphere, the cone, and the cylinder' was widely quoted among painters and sculptors, partly because it was still fashionable to pay homage to nature (in the Art Nouveau tradition), even while you were patently trying to get away from the Art Nouveau *mystique*.

But the people who really understood the new spirit Le Corbusier was seeking were not the painters or the sculptors, but a small band of engineer-architects – a group of rather unsophisticated men who, believing in 'honesty', had decided that architectural expression needed to be completely overhauled if it was even to begin to reflect the new technology of our time. And the greatest of these honest men was Auguste Perret – the master of reinforced-concrete construction.

Le Corbusier went to work for Perret and stayed for fifteen months. 'I wonder whether anyone realizes today what a heroic part Perret played in those years,' Corbu wrote in 1929. 'Perret had the temerity to build in [exposed] reinforced concrete, and he insisted that this new

structural method was destined to revolutionize our architecture.'
Perret had the temerity, and the instinct, to do much more: he took a
plastic material at a time when plasticity to excess was the mode, and
forced it into a classical discipline of restraint which, he knew, offered
the only rational solution to the most urgent problems of his time –
the building of tall structures, lightly framed and infinitely flexible
in plan.

Although Perret is today admired largely for what he did, he should
be praised as much for what he did not do. In the mud-building
countries around the edge of the Mediterranean, highly plastic, almost
sculptural architecture – whether in clay, stucco, or concrete – is the
tradition. These pliant materials present a tremendous temptation to
the architect, and few outside the classical tradition were able to resist
that temptation when Art Nouveau came along and made plasticity
respectable by relating it to forms in nature. Most of the great Art
Nouveau architects, from Antonio Gaudí in Barcelona to Victor
Horta in Brussels, surrendered to the voluptuous plasticity of concrete or the malleability of wrought iron. Auguste Perret and Tony
Garnier, his contemporary, were among the very few important
architects of their region and their time to insist upon architectural
logic in disciplining their concrete frames.

In wood-building countries like the United States the straight stick
and the equally straight board are the tradition; and the challenge is
to bend these straight sticks and boards into plastic forms. The great
Finnish architect Alvar Aalto met that challenge in his own wood-
building country in the 1930s, and Frank Lloyd Wright, in the United
States, made plasticity and continuity the twin principles of his life's
work. But in France and in all the other countries of the Mediterranean basin the challenge is to discipline plasticity into order. Where
the excitement of a Wright house is in the degree to which Wright
succeeded in bending the stick, the excitement of a concrete building
by Perret was in the degree to which he succeeded in straightening out
and disciplining mud.

Le Corbusier was enormously lucky to meet and work for Perret
when he did. For Perret was destined, in his later years, to see in classical discipline an end in itself, and in his final work – especially in the
vast reconstruction of the port of Le Havre, after the Second World
War – Perret had become an elegant and somewhat dry classicist.
But in 1908 Perret was at the very peak of his career. His own office
was located in the building at 22 bis rue Franklin, the first tall, exposed,

reinforced-concrete frame structure he had built half a dozen years earlier. In this building Perret had managed to realize a number of major principles of structure and plan which his talented pupil could take as points of departure towards his own objectives.

The apartment house at 22 bis rue Franklin is nine storeys high. Its frame is unfinished reinforced concrete, clearly expressed on the façade and left completely undecorated. The grid of columns and beams is filled in almost entirely with glass, except for a few areas that are enclosed with panels of brickwork to meet special building-code restrictions in the area. In plan the building is quite open: the only fixed elements are the slender reinforced-concrete columns and certain stair-wells. Everything else is nonstructural and, hence, entirely flexible. On the ground floor, for example, which contained Perret's office, Le Corbusier could see before his eyes the astonishing spectacle of a tall building apparently held up on nothing except a very few slim posts; all walls, all interior partitions, were large sheets of glass, some transparent, others translucent. Here, in all likelihood, was Corbu's first encounter with the concept of *pilotis*, or stilts, holding up a tall building and liberating the space beneath it – a concept Corbu was to develop into a revolutionary principle of city planning, as well as civic art.

Several other aspects of this building fascinated Le Corbusier and influenced his later work: first was the manner in which Perret had recessed the ground floor behind the plane of the main façade and, conversely, cantilevered or projected the upper floors out beyond the glassy face of the street floor. By today's standards, Perret's effort in this respect seems a little timid; we are accustomed to seeing tall slab buildings, like Lever House, in New York, supported on a smaller, receding base. But in 1902, when Perret designed this structure, the accepted way of arranging the masses of a building was not unlike that of building a pyramid: start with a broad base at the bottom, and taper off to a fine point as the building rises to its full height. Perret's understanding of reinforced concrete – a material composed in exact proportions of steel strands that can resist enormous tension, and concrete bulk that can resist enormous compression – led him to realize that a homogeneous and organic framework of this sort could be arranged to stand like a tree: its foundations rooted in the ground, its trunk slender and strong, projecting out of the ground, and its greatest mass, the branches and foliage, spreading out in all directions at the top. 22 bis rue Franklin was the first tall building constructed

on this tree principle – the precise opposite of the pyramidal structure derived from massive stone-building. Again Le Corbusier took
note of the principle and determined to explore its potentialities still
further.

Another aspect of the apartment house which intrigued Corbu was
its roof garden. The two top floors were stepped back to form small
terraces, on which Perret placed evergreen poplars planted in boxes.
Again the Perret experiment seems timid by comparison with Corbu's
later grandiose roof structures. Yet the germ of the idea was there;
Perret, being a sober, if brilliant, engineer, could not be expected to
develop it much further. Le Corbusier could and did.

But the most daring aspect of this simple and modest apartment
structure was the manner in which Perret had exposed its brute
concrete frame. 'Decoration,' Perret used to say, 'always hides an
error in construction.' (Adolf Loos, one of Perret's Viennese contemporaries, was even more vehement on the subject; according to *him*,
decoration was 'a crime!') In any event, Perret's honesty of structural
expression was almost unprecedented among designers in concrete,
and most architects considered the approach beneath their dignity.
Le Corbusier recalls that one day in 1909 the professor in charge of
structural theory at the conservative Beaux Arts Academy was indis-
posed, and his place was taken by the chief engineer of the Paris
Métro. 'Gentlemen,' the chief engineer began, 'I intend to devote
this lecture to a description of a new method of construction known as
reinforced concrete . . .' He was unable to proceed further, for his
voice was drowned out by catcalls. One student asked whether the
Métro engineer took them 'for a lot of contractors', whereupon the
lecturer retreated into a timid discourse on wood-frame structures of
the Middle Ages.

The Beaux Arts did make Perret a professor in the early thirties,
by which time Perret and reinforced concrete had both become quite
respectable. Yet Perret's brand of honest radicalism was a rare sight
in the first decade of the century, both in France and elsewhere. It is
true that in 1908, when Corbu went to work for Perret, a warehouse of
exposed reinforced concrete was built for Montgomery Ward & Co.
in Chicago, and that other 'honest' work was being done in Vienna,
Berlin, and other cities. But, by and large, these structures were not
considered polite architecture; they were part of the inventory of
purely utilitarian buildings demanded by industry and commerce.
Because this was so, Le Corbusier and others found themselves more

and more attracted to utilitarian buildings, such as factories, since they seemed to provide the only outlet for their energies and convictions. One of the great architects who had found this to be the case was the German Peter Behrens; and Behrens's studio in Berlin was, therefore, a natural next stop in Corbu's educational development.

THREE

Several factors made Peter Behrens important and attractive to the new generation of dreamers to which Corbu belonged: first, Behrens had started as a painter and craftsman in the Art Nouveau manner, and had gone on to reject it. That placed him several steps ahead of men like Josef Hoffmann, who never quite succeeded in shaking off the decorative urge of the Art Nouveau. Second, Behrens had turned to the classical tradition for some of the discipline he found lacking in Art Nouveau. Finally, and most importantly, Behrens had concentrated more and more upon industrial work – factories and the like – and upon the design of the industrial products made in those factories.

For Behrens had become the chief architect for the A.E.G. – a sort of German equivalent of our General Electric. It was his job to design not only A.E.G.'s factories, but also many of A.E.G.'s lighting fixtures, the typography for use on stationery and signs, and many other details that today go under the broad heading of 'industrial design'. Behrens was, indeed, the first modern industrial designer, and he gave A.E.G.'s buildings and products the sort of 'corporate identity' through total design which is admired so much today in firms like Italy's Olivetti and the Container Corporation.

Behrens was a classicist – or a semi-classicist – only in his 'important' work, such as his Art Building at an exhibition in Oldenburg in 1905 (which consisted of a series of cubic pavilions symmetrically grouped upon a formal pedestal), and in his monumental German embassy in St Petersburg, done in 1913. This was still polite architecture and seemed to call for a polite expression; Behrens's industrial work for A.E.G. was considered by most of his contemporaries as the sort of thing you had to do to meet the office overhead. Yet it is Behrens's steel-and-glass Turbine factory for A.E.G., in particular, which has assured him a permanent place in architectural history.

Because of Behrens's preoccupation with utilitarian building, his studio became the centre of much advanced work and thinking in the years immediately preceding the First World War. To become a

Behrens apprentice was the ambition of many young would-be architects of Corbu's inclinations and convictions; and so, when Le Corbusier obtained a special fellowship from his former Academy at La Chaux-de-Fonds to study advanced arts and crafts in Germany, he left Perret's office and proceeded to Berlin to meet Behrens and to work in his studio.

During the five months Corbu spent in Behrens's studio, there occurred one of the most remarkable coincidences in the story of architecture. While Corbu was working there, two other young men turned out to be fellow apprentices; one was the young Ludwig Mies van der Rohe, son of a modest masonry contractor in Aix-La-Chapelle (Aachen); the other was Walter Gropius, the elegant scion of a well-to-do north German family of professionals and businessmen. Corbu was twenty-three; Mies was twenty-four; and Gropius was twenty-seven years old. Each of the young apprentices was to learn something very special from Behrens: Corbu was to learn about technical organization and about Machine Art; Mies was to learn about classicism; and Gropius was to learn about the potentialities of an industrial civilization – a lesson he was to apply with tremendous success at his Bauhaus school ten years later.

Both Gropius and Mies had started with Behrens several years earlier, and remained in his studio after Corbu moved on to his next stop – another brief stint with Hoffmann in Vienna. But for all three the period in Behrens's office was tremendously significant. Le Corbusier saw something in Behrens's product design, in particular, which he had vaguely understood for some time, and which was now being confirmed. 'Nobody today can deny the aesthetic which is disengaging itself from the creations of modern industry,' he announced several years later, undoubtedly thinking of some of the things he had first seen in Behrens's studio. 'It is in general artistic production that the style of an epoch is found and not, as is too often supposed, in certain productions of an ornamental kind . . ."

It is almost impossible to exaggerate the depth and profundity of the change this new faith in the man-made object represented in architectural thought and, especially, in Le Corbusier's fundamental approach. Corbu and others were driven into utilitarianism in building because the doors to polite architecture were closed to them. Yet Corbu and Mies and Gropius were and are artists, first and foremost: the functioning of a lighting fixture or a power station was not of *primary* interest to them; it was something that must be taken for granted, just as one takes for granted that a writer knows how to use a pen. The important thing to these men was the development of a new aesthetic language, and specifically a language that could be used to deal with the problems of today. In utilitarian buildings and products they found the aesthetic vocabulary – cubes, spheres, cylinders, cones, and so forth. In their purity and precision, these objects (which might happen to be salt shakers, meat grinders, or racing cars) represented a 'new look' – the look of what was later termed Machine Art. It was an exhilarating experience, the discovery of this vast new world of form. Amédée Ozenfant, the painter who was associated with Le Corbusier for several years after the First World War, once pointed out that it was much better to be a first-class engineer than a second-class artist, and added that Ettore Bugatti, who designed the most beautiful sports cars ever built, was obviously a much greater artist than his brother, the rather indifferent sculptor Rembrandt Bugatti!

Le Corbusier, Léger, and many other painters and scupltors were carried away by this same enthusiasm for Machine Art. They saw no need to justify among themselves this new vocabulary of forms: the forms were beautiful, they belonged to an orderly and coherent system, and that was all that really mattered. But *vis-à-vis* the lay public, they took a different position. Just as the Art Nouveau designers had justified their point of view by suggesting that (a) nature is 'honest' (whatever that may mean) and therefore (b) forms taken from nature must be 'honest' too, so Corbu and his fellow enthusiasts felt compelled to argue that (a) machines are efficient and therefore (b) forms borrowed from machines must be efficient too. Nobody except, perhaps, the nineteenth-century American sculptor Horatio Greenough (Emerson's friend) ever really believed this; but the notion caught on like wildfire and 'functionalism' in architecture was born. Almost everyone was willing to accept buildings they considered ugly if those 'ugly' buildings were indeed less expensive to build and more efficient to operate. The functionalists were stuck with their machine analogy – and are stuck with it to this day.

The discovery of a new world of geometric forms affected Corbu in another profound way. He and his contemporaries considered themselves in revolt, not only against eclecticism, but against the pseudo-naturalism of Art Nouveau as well. Specifically, Le Corbusier – now a firm believer in the man-made object – became something of an anti-naturalist. 'The city,' he said, 'is man's grip upon nature. It is a human operation directed against nature.' To him the idea of integrating architecture and nature, in the manner of Art Nouveau and, later, of Frank Lloyd Wright, became anathema. A building must be a clear, sophisticated statement, he felt, and it should stand in contrast to nature, rather than appear as an outgrowth of some natural formation. Nature and architecture could enhance one another in this manner and create a sort of harmony by contrast. The concept, of course, was not new: the Greeks believed in it and made their Acropolis a man-made crown to top off a mountain. To Corbu this approach to nature seemed somehow more truly respectful than the emulation of natural forms as practised by Gaudí or Guimard.

By the time Corbu left Behrens's studio late in 1910, he had made certain clear-cut decisions for himself – decisions that changed very little during the decades that followed. First, he was committed, completely and irrevocably, to the new world of form which the Cubists had begun to paint and which the architect-engineers of Perret's and Behrens's stripe had begun to manipulate. Second, he was committed to a *laissez-faire* attitude towards nature: he believed that nature should be left to her natural devices, and that architecture should be the prerogative of men. Third, he was committed to reinforced concrete, not only because this seemed the obvious modern material of France, but also because it appeared to possess a certain amount of plain ' guts', which he, being of the Mediterranean tradition, preferred to the impersonal slickness and precision of steel. And, finally, he was committed to the tradition of the Mediterranean – not the rehashed tradition as interpreted by the Beaux Arts, but the strength and vigour and grandeur of Greece and Rome and the Renaissance. After his stay in Germany, he said that there was a great deal the French could learn from German technology, but that there was an absence among the Germans of certain traditions. Their hands, he said, seemed to be rather clumsy, unlike (he might have added) the hands of the fishermen-builders of the coasts of Greece and Italy and Spain.

In the years that remained before the outbreak of the First World War Corbu increased his knowledge of the traditions of the Mediterranean basin. For more than a year he travelled through the Balkans, in Asia Minor, in the Greek Islands (including especially Mykonos), and in Italy. His sketchbooks of this trip – like those of his earlier travels – contain not only the obvious, though beautifully rendered impressions of Pisa, Pompeii, the Acropolis, the Piazza San Marco, but also some fascinating details of a stone wall, a cluster of trees in a Middle East market place, a plan of a Roman house, the distant silhouette of a small Italian hill town. When he returned to La Chaux-de-Fonds, Le Corbusier's basic education was complete.

Three events of major importance in the history of modern architecture took place in Europe during the years immediately preceding the First World War. The most important of these, in all likelihood, was the publication of a book – or, rather, of two books: the 1910 and 1911 editions of the Berlin publisher Wasmuth's *Executed Buildings and Projects by Frank Lloyd Wright*. In connexion with the first of the two Wasmuth publications, an exhibition of Wright's work also came to Berlin. Mies van der Rohe remembers the occasion well. 'Wright's work presented an architectural world of unexpected force, clarity of language, and disconcerting richness of form,' Mies has said. It is easy to see what Mies and his contemporaries found disconcerting; for, unlike them, Wright had never been won over to the pure geometry of machine forms. Instead, his architecture contained, from the start, a certain exuberance that was typically Art Nouveau – or, perhaps, even more typically American. This richness of detail and of form was all the more disconcerting to the Machine Art men because they had just discovered another sort of American building which seemed to strengthen their own purist position: the great silos, bridges, and docks constructed by American engineers. They fully expected that any 'modern' American architect would inevitably be a Machine Art man too. Certainly Wright's monumentally simple Larkin building of 1904 must have appealed to any disciple of Peter Behrens; but Wright's decorative detail in such buildings as the Coonley house of 1908 ran directly counter to all Machine Art thought.

A second event of tremendous importance was the design and construction of two buildings, in 1911 and 1914 respectively, by Walter Gropius in association with Adolph Meyer. These two structures were the only completely 'modern' buildings (in our sense today) erected in Europe before 1914. In their over-all concept and in many details these buildings seem so advanced that a layman, coming upon them unprepared today, would almost certainly date them in the middle 1930s or even later. Unfortunately, of the two buildings only one has survived the wars.

The first of these extraordinary structures was the Fagus factory, built for a manufacturer of shoe lasts. It was Gropius's first large commission, and he left Behren's office to undertake it The main portion of this building was a three-storey cage of brick, steel, and glass, as completely and uncompromisingly 'modern' as Mies van der Rohe's glass-and-steel campus for the Illinois Institute of Technology, started in 1940, almost thirty years later. The glass façades of the Fagus factory were among the first completely modern 'curtain walls' – skins or membranes stretched tautly over the structural framework of the building behind the glass. Not even Behrens, in his Turbine factory, had so completely expressed the separation of the glass skin from the steel skeleton; in the Turbine factory the corners were still massively of concrete, whereas in Gropius's structure the corners had, in effect, been dissolved in a knife-edged line of two planes of glass meeting on a thin steel edge-strip. The Fagus factory has now been made a 'historic monument', protected by the laws of the Bonn Republic, and continues to function perfectly.

The 1914 building was Gropius's contribution to the Cologne exhibition of the Deutsche Werkbund, an association of artists, workers, and industrialists dedicated to the production of objects of high aesthetic quality. His administrative office building for the exhibition again presented a sheer, seemingly weightless 'curtain wall' of glass, hung from the structural framework; in addition, the building contained two glass-enclosed spiral staircases of reinforced concrete – a device that was much admired and imitated by modern architects for decades to come. Oddly enough, the Werkbund building also betrayed certain touches of Wrightian detail, particularly in the sweeping roof overhangs. No such influence was evident in the Fagus factory; but whether Gropius was indeed influenced by Wright in the design of this exhibition building is questionable. There is no question, however, that Gropius was still somewhat under the influence of Behrens's classicism when he designed the Fagus and the Werkbund buildings: both have a rather classical base; both retain certain semi-classical details around entrances; and both are largely symmetrical – as, indeed, were most of Frank Lloyd Wright's early buildings. Still, even with these few, somewhat traditional touches, Gropius's two buildings represented so radical, so complete a break with the past that their construction must have had the effect of a violent explosion in the world of architecture. So great was their impact that several architects of considerable reputation built a large part of their life's work upon further development of the Fagus and Werkbund themes. The Werkbund building, incidentally, was destroyed in the First World War.

The third event that shaped the development of modern architecture in general, and of Le Corbusier in particular, took place in painting and sculpture in the years before the First World War. In their Cubist paintings both Picasso and Braque had begun to portray people and objects in such a way that several sides of the model, animate or inanimate, were visible simultaneously. In Futurist sculpture and painting – a school particularly strong in Italy – the concept of movement became paramount: objects and figures were shown not in a single, static position, but while in motion. Marcel Duchamp, though not a Futurist himself, expressed the idea in his famous *Nude Descending the Staircase* – a figure shown actually in motion, much as it might appear if several successive movie frames had been projected simultaneously upon the same screen.

What all this meant to architecture was the possibility of exploring a new and different kind of space – a space not bottled up in cubicles, not statically contained within four walls, a floor, and a roof, but a space experienced simultaneously from without and within, seen by the observer in passing through, rather than frozen to a single spot in the total composition. In a different sort of way Frank Lloyd Wright had made a similar discovery of space-in-motion a few years earlier, but his kind of space was, fundamentally, horizontal. The spatial discoveries made by the Cubists and the Futurists were both more formalized and more all-enveloping – up, down, sideways, back, and front, all at the same time.

Gropius's glass-sheathed buildings, in which there was, in effect, no visual separation between the indoors and the outdoors, paralleled the space-in-motion theories developed by the painters and sculptors. But Corbu was to advance the theme still further in architecture: he would hollow out parts of the cube to create outdoor space within his buildings, and, at the same time, enclose part of the outdoors to create clearly defined 'rooms' *outside* his buildings; moreover, he would make his buildings not only objects to be seen in a horizontal plane, but objects in the round, meant to be seen from underneath and from above, from all sides and from inside – and let each view suggest all the other views.

Meanwhile, the painters and sculptors taught Corbu something rather obvious: that it was much easier, in certain ways, to conduct experiments in spatial and formal organization by means of painting and sculpture than by means of full-scale architecture. For one thing, it was certainly cheaper; for another, there was no client and there were no functional limitations. So, when the war came, Le Corbusier returned to La Chaux-de-Fonds to paint, to teach, and to think. 'Today painting has outsped the other arts,' Corbu said. 'It is the first to have become attuned with our epoch . . . Far removed from a distracting realism, it lends itself to meditation . . . After the day's work it is good to meditate.'

Being Swiss by nationality, Corbu was not directly involved in the
First World War, and so he found much time to meditate; but, being
French by inclination, Corbu tended to 'meditate' in ways that are
characteristic of the French.

Compare what happened to Machine Art in the hands of the
German pioneers – and what happened to Machine Art in the hands
of Le Corbusier. In Germany, needless to say, the argument that
because the machine was efficient, any architecture derived from
Machine Art must therefore be functional in the extreme, found ready
adherents everywhere. But in France the basic premise of this argument was immediately recognized for the fallacy it contained: as
every Frenchman knows, machines hardly ever work; as every
Frenchman also knows, French machines, while particularly erratic,
are invariably much more beautiful than machines produced in
any other country. The French, being the most humorous nation on
earth, never really took their machines as seriously as did the Germans
(or, for that matter, the English, the Americans, or the Russians).
Machines were beautiful toys: only in France could one expect to
find as lovely a piece of madness as the famous Pont Transbordeur,
which spanned the entrance to the Vieux Port of Marseille.

This fantastic suspension bridge consisted of two tall towers with
an elevated roadway between them; the roadway was used by small
trolleys that shuttled back and forth between the ends of the bridge;
and, suspended from these trolleys by cables, were little ferry boats
that, in turn, shuttled back and forth from one side of the Vieux Port
to the other as the trolleys moved back and forth high above them.
Now, to a German engineer, it might have seemed a little simpler to
operate an ordinary ferry service between the two sides of the harbour
without benefit of superstructure; and, indeed, the German com-
mandant of Marseille, in the Second World War, was so infuriated
by this delightful piece of nonsense that he had the Pont Transbordeur
melted down for scrap. Yet, to the French, it was equally obvious

that the *poetic* solution to this engineering problem demanded exactly the lovely sort of structure erected at Marseille.

The important thing about Le Corbusier's conception of Machine Art was that the emphasis was on the word 'Art'. All his talk about functionalism, his later and oft-quoted insistence that 'a house is a machine for living in', means only two things: first, that he felt compelled to 'sell' his ideas to an unsympathetic public in terms other than those of pure art; and, second, that he was primarily saying that 'a house should be as *beautiful* as a machine', not necessarily as efficient as an A.E.G. generator.

This does not mean that Corbu was or is against functionalism; it only means that functionalism has never interested him as much as his so-called humanist critics have alleged. Undoubtedly a painter needs to know something about the chemistry of pigments; but knowing this does not make him a good painter. As a matter of fact, Corbu's buildings, generally, have been very well built; in many of them he has introduced technical innovations of major importance. For example, the grilles of sun-control devices now so fashionable in certain kinds of modern architecture were pioneered by Corbu several decades before others were able to turn them into a personal 'trademark' or publicity stunt. But, by and large, Corbu has been less concerned with the technology of architecture than with its art. The confusion about Corbu's true objectives stems from the single, simple fact that he found his major sources of *aesthetic* inspiration in the *technology* of our time.

In his own way Le Corbusier tried to make this point quite clear in his paintings done during the war years and afterwards. Like the Cubists, Corbu chose the most uninteresting objects he could find – bottles, pipes, violins, cups, and saucers – so as to avoid distraction from the basic theme of the painting, which was the arrangement of pure, geometric, Machine Art forms like cylinders, cubes, cones, and spheres. The literary images in the painting were decidedly incidental; it was the formal quality of each object which interested Corbu. When Gertrude Stein said that 'a rose is a rose is a rose', she meant that a rose is an object of beauty with inherent qualities of its own, not a symbol of something else, like love, or sentiment, or early summer. In his paintings Le Corbusier said, in effect, that 'a cube is a cube is a cube' – and never mind what the cube (or cylinder or sphere) might happen to represent. 'Eyes that do not see' became one of Corbu's most insistent laments about his contemporaries;

what he was trying to re-create in his paintings and drawings was the appreciation of forms for their own sake, and, specifically, the appreciation of a new order of forms.

Le Corbusier returned to Paris in 1917, to stay. He moved into a studio at 20 rue Jacob, where he was to remain for the next seventeen years. Shortly thereafter he met the painter Amédée Ozenfant. It was one of Corbu's many partnerships with men and women of creative vision, and it lasted until 1925, when the two broke up their association – as, indeed, most of Corbu's later associations were to break up. Ozenfant, a Cubist, possessed something Le Corbusier had great difficulty in finding elsewhere: he had eyes that *did* see! Corbu wrote to him: 'Of those I know, you are the one who seems to be carrying out most clearly what is stirring within me . . .' Several months later Corbu and Ozenfant jointly signed a manifesto entitled *Après le cubisme*, which suggested that while Cubism had cleared the air by removing the most distracting elements of realism from painting, it had now degenerated into a sort of playful, romantic, decorative movement. Corbu and Ozenfant proposed to return to the rational, geometric foundations of Cubism, and began a new movement within the Cubist tradition which they named Purism. Their first joint exhibition of paintings took place in 1918, at the Galerie Thomas, and from that time on, for the next several years, Corbu (known then by his original name, Jeanneret) and Ozenfant were more or less inseparable. Together with the poet Paul Dermée they began, in October 1920, to publish a magazine they called *L'Esprit nouveau*, devoted to all the plastic arts, to architecture, engineering, music, writing, industrial design, and 'l'esthétique de la vie moderne'. That just about covered everything, and *L'Esprit nouveau* was, indeed, an extraordinarily lively and broad review, whose influence could hardly be exaggerated. The magazine itself folded three years and twenty-eight issues after it was founded, but the term *L'Esprit nouveau* continued as a kind of trademark for much of Corbu's later work. And most of his books in the twenties and thirties were published under the *L'Esprit nouveau* imprint.

A collection of statements on architecture which had appeared in *L'Esprit nouveau* were republished in 1923 by Le Corbusier in a book entitled *Vers une architecture* – the most important book produced by this prolific writer and one of the most influential books to have been written by a European architect since the inception of the modern movement. Ozenfant has claimed that *Vers une architecture* was largely a rewrite of articles jointly produced for *L'Esprit nouveau* by himself and Corbu; however that may be, the book came out under Corbu's name alone, and its publication was the beginning of a certain coolness between Corbu and Ozenfant. The book is primarily concerned with architecture; it lays down, with almost frightening prescience, certain principles according to which Le Corbusier has lived and worked ever since; and whether or not he was responsible for every word of the text, he has, in his life's work, given substance to each word of that text, and thus made the book one of the great manifestos in the history of art.

The publication of *Vers une architecture* marked a milestone both in the development of modern architecture and in Corbu's own life. From that date, Le Corbusier stopped exhibiting his paintings (he was tired of being known as a painter and a sort of 'dilettante architect') and stopped using the name Jeanneret. He continued to paint, of course; but he wanted to be known primarily – even exclusively – as an architect, and he refused to show any of his other work until many years later, in 1937. By that time Corbu had radically altered the architectural face of the twentieth century, and no one could possibly accuse him of dilettantism.

'A great epoch has begun! There exists a new spirit!' That is how Le Corbusier opened his *Vers une architecture*. No one but the French should be permitted to make revolutions; only they know how to compose the necessary manifestos. Throughout *Vers une architecture* there is this same revolutionary fervour – the emotional appeal, the audible rolling of drums. This was heady stuff. It was the beginning of Corbu's poetic vision of architecture.

Never has architecture been more beautifully defined. '*L'architecture est le jeu savant, correct et magnifique des volumes assemblés sous la lumière*,' Corbu wrote. In the English translation, published four years after *Vers une architecture* appeared in France, his words lose some of their passion. 'Architecture is the masterly, correct and magnificent play of masses brought together in light.' And Corbu continued: 'Our eyes are made to see forms in light: cubes, cones, spheres, cylinders, or pyramids are the great primary forms.' The statement was, of course accompanied by the now standard photographs of American grain elevators and silos, bridges, docks, ships, and aeroplanes. 'The engineer, inspired by the laws of economy and governed by mathematical calculation, puts us in accord with universal law,' Corbu wrote. But, almost in the same breath, he made it absolutely clear that to him, at least, functionalism was *not* architecture. 'Architecture goes beyond utilitarian needs,' he said. And then: '*Passion can create drama out of inert stone*.'

It is hard to understand how so many of Corbu's critics could fail to see Corbu for what he was and is: a hopeless romantic, a dreamer, a passionate lover of architecture as man's most noble form of self-expression. Naturally Corbu's romanticism is of an order very different from that of Wright or of the latter-day Arts-and-Crafts enthusiasts in California and elsewhere. For his is a romanticism born not out of the American prairie or out of the Japanese garden, but out of the greatness of the Mediterranean – out of the greatness of its particular and fabulous tradition. To Corbu the silo is today's Luxor, today's temple at Thebes, today's Parthenon. The 'masses brought together in light' are the cylinders and spheres of Ancient Egypt, Greece, and Rome, of the Renaissance, as much as the cylinders and spheres of today's power stations and ocean liners. And if he believes in a 'spirit of order, a unity of intention', then he is not speaking as a modern totalitarian (as certain American critics have stated), but as the heir to a tradition of laws without which democracy would never have had a chance to function in the first place.

Vers une architecture was not only a tract on aesthetics, it was a statement about the all-encompassing role of architecture as Corbu saw it. Although it started with a denunciation of eclecticism – of the revived 'styles' – and went on to offer a modern alternative, this was merely the beginning of an extraordinarily broad definition of architecture. For here, in his first major book, Corbu showed himself not just as another partisan of modern art and modern architecture, but as an impressive social commentator, critic, and philosopher of his time.

The new 'machine aesthetic' led him, naturally, to a rationalization of the effect of the machine upon the production of architecture. With supreme clarity he discussed the problems and opportunities of mass production in building, recognizing that such mass production would mean adherence to certain dimensional standards. This fact had, of course, been understood by others before Corbu, but he went beyond the then widely accepted need for standardization by making two significant points: first, Corbu suggested that the objective of standardization imposed upon every architect a sort of moral obligation to design *only* in a vocabulary that might, some day, fit into a mass-production grammar. In other words, he made it quite clear that the time for individual, egocentric expression in architecture had passed, and that the only architectural statement of any validity or significance was one that pointed directly towards a broader solution. And, second, Corbu went back to the traditional Renaissance rules of measure and proportion for a guide to some sort of modern unit system. Specifically, he analysed the 'Golden Section' – the famous proportional system of old – and suggested that it was as valid today as it was when used in the design of Notre-Dame.

The significance of Le Corbusier's insistence upon a *proportional* system of measurement has been widely overlooked. While others recognized the need for what is now called a modular system of design – i.e., a system based upon the repetition of *identically* dimensioned units – Corbu realized from the very start that a system based upon a 1 plus 1 plus 1 plus 1 rhythm (*ad infinitum*) could only lead to monotony. (Every New Yorker looking at the 1 plus 1 plus 1 plus 1 glass-and-metal 'wallpaper' that has sprung up around him since 1945 knows exactly what Corbu had in mind.) To avoid this deadly sort of monotony, Corbu felt that a system not of identical units but of *related proportions* was the answer to the mass production of building parts. The Greeks' 'Golden Section' represented a possible approach; it took him twenty years to develop a more refined system – a system he has called the Modulor – to serve the needs of mass production today. Those needs, as he saw them from the start, were to facilitate prefabrication while avoiding repetitive monotony. The Modulor, with its proportionate scale, makes possible an infinite number of variations within a unit system of construction. In 1958, when Corbu began to build the Dominican monastery of La Tourette near Lyon, he used the Modulor to determine the spacing of his window divisions, and the result was a façade that was vibrant with movement, and ever changing in the light. '*Le jeu savant, correct et magnifique . . . sous la lumière . . .*'

But Corbu went far beyond his aesthetic analyses, far beyond the analysis of function, of plan, of structure, of prefabrication. To him it was clear that architecture in the twentieth century could no longer be the isolated building, the individual house (or even the individual skyscraper). *The city as a whole was architecture*: its basic organization, its spatial relationships, its forms, its levels of activity, its heart – all these seemed to Corbu of supreme significance, of much greater importance even than the development (or absence) of a style.

It is very likely that Corbu was influenced, in his concepts of city planning, by two earlier visionary ideas: the Cité Industrielle, suggested as early as 1901 by Tony Garnier, the enthusiastic exponent of reinforced concrete; and a somewhat similar notion developed by Corbu's old master, Auguste Perret, in an interview with a correspondent from the Paris *L'Intransigeant*. Garnier's ideal city of 35,000 inhabitants was based upon a network of transportation arteries, with each type of transport separately provided for. The core of Garnier's city was a large civic centre, and there were separate areas for industry, commerce, residential use, health, etc. Perret's idea was to build a city of isolated towers spaced far apart. In certain ways Perret had turned the principles embodied in his apartment building on the rue Franklin into a city pattern: the street level was to be open

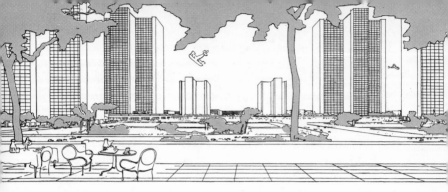

2. View from a terrace-restaurant into the Ville Contemporaine, 1922.
(*From* Œuvre complète)

to through traffic, the residential areas were to be located in the tower floors above, and the roof was to be a garden space.

Le Corbusier took these two concepts and made them rational, modern, and beautiful. A year before *Vers une architecture* was published, he designed a 'City for Three Million Inhabitants', which was exhibited in November 1922 at the Salon d'Automne in Paris. This project, in almost every detail, laid down the principles of city planning to which Corbu has subscribed ever since. It has been widely (and ignorantly) attacked ever since it was first publicized; and yet no city planner in Europe, the Americas, or Asia has come up with a clearer, more rational, more 'human', or more beautiful proposal for a large metropolis in the thirty or forty years since Corbu first developed his scheme.

The 1922 Ville Contemporaine [2 and 3] was, of course, a diagram and never intended to be anything but a diagram. Its most important features were these: all fast automobile traffic was to be handled by a few elevated highways, never crossed by a pedestrian. These elevated highways crisscrossed the city, made its centre easily and quickly accessible, and were joined at their ends by a peripheral highway system that bypassed the city altogether. (By 1956 Philadelphia, Fort Worth, and other cities had finally decided to adopt substantially the same system to solve their apparently insoluble downtown traffic congestion.) Meanwhile, all pedestrian traffic was to take place on the normal ground level, on streets and walks threaded through open parks and gardens. As most of the buildings were to be elevated on stilts, or *pilotis*, pedestrians were free to walk anywhere, everywhere, and without the slightest danger.

The centre of Corbu's Ville Contemporaine was to be a group of skyscrapers, cruciform in plan, fifty or sixty storeys in height, and spaced very far apart to permit the development of generous park spaces between them [2]. The cruciform towers were to contain offices for the administration of the city, for business and the professions. A civic centre was to be located near by.

The next 'ring' in this pattern – the Ville Contemporaine actually consisted of a series of concentric, rectangular belts – was a development of apartment houses, each of them six 'double storeys' in height. These apartment houses were to be built in the form of long, continuous 'walls', wandering in and out, changing direction, and thus creating spacious garden courts and parks for the use of the apartment dwellers. As these buildings were to be raised on *pilotis* as well, there was free movement between adjoining courts underneath and through the various structures.

3. Plan for a City of Three Million Inhabitants, 1922. The street pattern combines the American gridiron system with the radial plan of Paris. (From Œuvre complète)

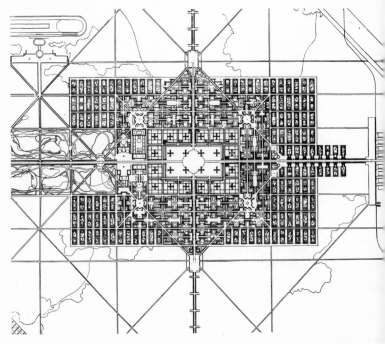

Finally, there was to be an outer ring of garden apartments of a very special sort – Corbu called them *villas superposées* – which were to be grouped around inner courts laid out as recreation areas. These villas will be described in some detail later on; it is enough to say now that here again Le Corbusier anticipated our very latest housing concepts by more than a generation.

The Ville Contemporaine was to be protected by a massive belt of greenery, several miles thick, beyond which would be located industrial districts, perhaps a port, a great sports arena, or a small suburb of individual houses.

Two aspects of this project seem particularly impressive today: first, that this is in many respects the basis for every radical 'new' city being discussed seriously anywhere in the world today; and, second, that in this one project Le Corbusier, with a precision of mind rarely equalled by artists in any field, outlined exactly what he planned to do during the years ahead. Since 1922 Corbu has given life – bones, muscles, flesh, blood, and, above all, heart – to the exquisite and delicate drawings prepared in that year; but he has never deviated very far from the basic principles established in the Ville Contemporaine and in *Vers une architecture*.

SEVEN

In retrospect today, it seems odd that Corbu's *Vers une architecture* attracted as much attention as it did when it appeared. The fact is that before 1923 Le Corbusier had built almost nothing: apart from the early villa at La Chaux-de-Fonds, a commission that enabled him to take his first series of trips outside Switzerland, he had barely completed two small houses: one at Vaucresson; the other – a studio for Ozenfant – in Paris. Although they were exciting for their time in their simplicity, in the use of the 'open plan' and of rectangular as well as more plastic forms, these two houses do not measure up to the standards he was soon to set in more mature buildings.

Nor did these houses measure up, entirely, to the quality of Le Corbusier's many proposals developed during the war years and after. It was these proposals (of which the Ville Contemporaine was the most important) that attracted people's attention to Le Corbusier and gave him the audience he deserved when his book appeared.

Among the projects of the war and postwar years, there were two that stood out, in addition to the City Plan: his design for the Dom-ino houses in 1914 [4], and his project for the Citrohan house in

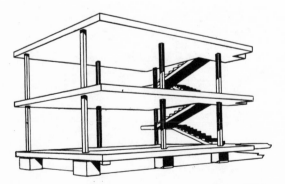

4. *Column-and-slab structure for Dom-ino houses, 1914.*
(*From* Œuvre complete)

1922. Dom-ino was a simple statement about the possibilities of reinforced-concrete construction: a frame of six columns, supporting all floor and roof slabs, with a cantilevered stair linking the different levels to the ground and the roof. These structural elements were the only fixed parts of the house; everything else was nonstructural and hence entirely flexible. It was a clear and convincing statement of the 'open plan' – a plan freed from the need of load-bearing walls and hence capable of infinite variation within the same structural system.

The Citrohan house [5] was a much more sophisticated affair. Here was the first development of one of Corbu's major spatial ideas: the creation of interlocking spaces of different but related heights. The house was two storeys high. It had two floor levels on one side, with the kitchen and the dining area on the lower level, and bedrooms on the upper floor. The living area, however, was a double-storey room, its floor on the same level as the kitchen and dining areas, its ceiling an extension of the bedroom ceilings upstairs. A spiral stair connected the living level to the sleeping areas and formed a sculptural counterpoint to the severe, rectilinear geometry of the hollow cube

5. One version of the Citrohan house concept, developed by Le Corbusier between 1922 and 1927. All houses are on stilts and have a roof patio. (From Œuvre complète)

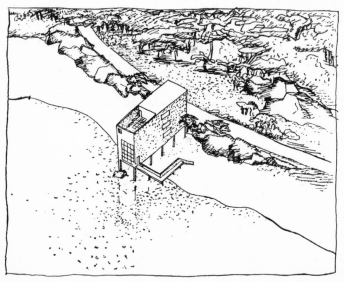

that was the interior. The flat roof was treated as an elaborate garden, with guest-rooms located in a small penthouse superstructure.

This basic idea – the two-to-one interior space – has been a recurrent theme in all of Le Corbusier's work ever since Citrohan. In keeping with his conviction that every design, however small, must make a contribution to the solution of a wider, more general problem of architecture, he used the Citrohan two-to-one scheme as a kind of laboratory for an apartment prototype he was to develop further in his Ville Contemporaine a couple of years later, and still further in years to come. It is an exciting spatial concept, giving each apartment (or terrace house unit) a tall, studiolike living area contrasted with service rooms of lower ceiling height. In the *villas superposées* for his Ville Contemporaine, Corbu extended this spatial idea to the outdoors as well and provided each of the 'superimposed houses' not only with a two-storey living-room *but also with a two-storey garden terrace punched out of the building at regular intervals* [6]. Here is a truly radical concept of urban living – a concept that is only just being accepted by a very few architects in this country: the idea that a private garden-in-the-sky can be provided for every family even in a so-called tower apartment unit. In aesthetic terms this creation of hollow outdoor cubes within the building volume

6. *Portion of an apartment house consisting of 'superimposed villas', 1922. Each living unit has a two-storey-high 'garden-in-the-sky'.* (*From* Œuvre complète)

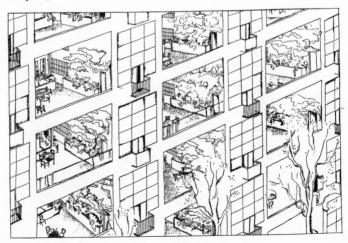

exactly parallels the Cubist attempt to make objects visible simultaneously from several sides and directions. Corbu's two-to-one, indoor-outdoor spaces suggested a spatial advance beyond that of the 'open plan' developed by Wright and others – an advance beyond the horizontal movement of space and into the vertical dimension.

Citrohan's roof garden, as well as the roof gardens on the apartment buildings in his Ville Contemporaine, are steps beyond Perret's somewhat timid indication in the apartment house on rue Franklin. The roof garden (as opposed to the punched-out private garden next to each apartment) was conceived of as a communal space, a kind of elevated piazza for the use of all the inhabitants of the building. And Corbu began, almost immediately, to treat the roof garden as an architectural space: a plaza animated by forms (both of architecture and of plantings) which would give its space light and shade, life and scale. At Citrohan the penthouse was merely a smaller cube placed on the larger cube of the house proper; but before long he carried this concept beyond its initial stage and gave the roof garden a distinct visual enclosure – the form of an outdoor room open to the sky.

7. Sketch for an ideal apartment produced by Le Corbusier in the 1930s. Its use of two interlocking levels was prophetic of his Marseille apartments and those that followed. (From Œuvre complète)

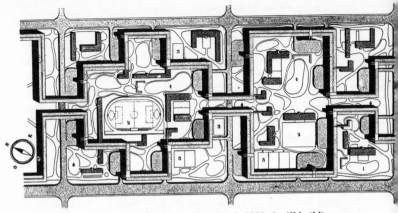

8. *Garden apartments in an ideal 'Radiant City'. 1930–6. All buildings were to be built on stilts so that pedestrians could circulate freely at ground level. Automobile traffic is on elevated highways. The architectural pattern is geometric, but the pattern of pedestrian paths and landscaping is very free.* (*From* Œuvre complete)

In these sketches Corbu had, in effect, developed almost all of his tall-building concepts – developed them in microcosm, as it were. The best way to understand what he had done is to think of a typical small French street, the sort of street Maurice Utrillo loved to paint. The street is the public circulation artery; it is lined with high walls that, in turn, are punctured at regular intervals by doorways and gates. Behind these walls is a series of enclosed, very private patios, one for each family. And within each patio stands a house, an enclosed living-space. At the far end of the street there is, generally, a small public plaza, a place where the inhabitants of the street may gather and conduct whatever social functions are conducted outdoors. This is the communal outdoor space, as differentiated from the private outdoor space represented by each of the small patios.

In essence, Corbu proposed to stand this traditional French street up on its end: the street was now a vertical circulation shaft (elevators, fire stairs, and so forth). At each level there were entrance doors into single-family 'houses', the patio being the garden-in-the-sky, the house being the enclosed living-space available to each family. And, at the end of the circulation shaft, on the roof, there was the public plaza, the outdoor space within which the inhabitants along the vertical street could meet to talk and to watch their children play.

Le Corbusier realized from the start that he had to go up, and that the only way to preserve any park spaces worth talking about was to go up very high, and to locate his towers very far apart. One result of this was bound to be a rather detached attitude towards nature – detached in fact as well as in spirit. While Frank Lloyd Wright was trying to dig in and, literally, get under nature's skin, Corbu tried to divorce his buildings from the ground as much as possible to keep that ground free from man-made obstacles, and to use some of the elements of nature, such as trees and shrubs, as architectural forms lifted out of their natural habitat and plunked down on terraces and roof gardens where they might form a pleasant diversion.

As Le Corbusier refined the basic idea of a vertical street, he included shops along the street as well; these became shopping levels half-way up the building, as in the apartment building he completed in 1952, at Marseille. And he incorporated in his public plaza certain enclosed communal spaces, such as nursery schools, gymnasiums, cinemas, and restaurants. The public plaza on the roof became a social and cultural centre of major importance.

In plastic expression, he began to differentiate between the repetitive patterns of the 'street' and the unique structures required by the public plaza. The 'street' and its 'houses' – i.e., the apartments – tended to form a tall, rectangular slab subdivided more or less regularly into apartment units; but the 'plaza' on the roof became an increasingly free composition of curvilinear forms, a huge sculpture garden designed as a counterpoint to the simplicity of the slab, just as his interior spiral stairs and sculptural fireplaces were designed to provide counterpoints to the geometry of the cubic space in which they stood.

Although most of this did not become reality until much later, Corbu rarely designed or built anything in the twenties that did not in some manner contribute to his central idea of a vertical city. It is almost incredible today to see Le Corbusier's singleness of purpose throughout these years: however small the project, however far removed it may have appeared from what he considered to be his central mission, there was hardly a line drawn in his office which did not elaborate upon that mission. In the double house for La Roche and Albert Jeanneret (a brother), designed in 1923, there is the first actual use of the *pilotis* to elevate a portion of the building and thus permit a continuous garden space at ground level; there are several interlocking one- and two-storey high spaces, connected again by means of sculptural stairs and bridges; there is the first actual execution of a roof garden treated as a plastic counterpoint; and there is an attempt to rationalize the entire building by subordinating its design to some sort of proportionate scale.

In 1925 Le Corbusier and his cousin, Pierre Jeanneret, with whom he had become associated in all his architectural work, were commissioned to design and build an advanced housing development in Pessac, near Bordeaux. As this was to be located in a suburban area, there was no reason to use vertical structures; but Corbu's solution of terrace houses with completely developed roof gardens, patios, and open ground floors was simply a horizontal variation upon the same theme.

Here at Pessac, as in many other places, Le Corbusier was to run head-on into violent opposition on the part of various authorities, and his buildings stood vacant for more than three years after they were completed because some benighted local bureaucrats, who objected to the uncompromising geometry of Corbu's open and closed cubes, refused to issue the necessary occupancy permits. Le Corbusier noted wryly that it took less than one year to construct the Pessac buildings, but that it took more than three years, plus the intervention of two high government officials from Paris, to get the necessary occupancy documents signed!

EIGHT

Throughout the 1920s Le Corbusier concentrated upon the further development of this one basic theme: the hollowed-out cube (which he called a 'pure prism'), generally raised on *pilotis* and topped with a roof garden whose forms were suggestive of sculpture. In the course of this development, he built half a dozen houses of great beauty and strength.

The first of these was not, strictly speaking, a house at all. It was a pavilion – the Pavillon de l'Esprit Nouveau [9] – designed by him and Jeanneret for the International Exhibition of Decorative Arts,

9. Pavillon de l'Esprit Nouveau, 1925. This exhibition structure is actually an apartment unit similar to one of the 'superimposed villas' designed in 1922. (Courtesy, Museum of Modern Art)

held in Paris in 1925. The pavilion was a full-size model of one of the two-storey 'superimposed villas' Corbu had developed a couple of years earlier for his Ville Contemporaine. There was a two-storey garden space (a hollow, outdoor cube), closed off on two sides by a typical two-storey apartment, complete with a two-storey living-room.

Here, as at Pessac, Corbu was to meet a degree of hostility hard to imagine today. While there is still, of course, a good deal of opposition to the sort of work done by Le Corbusier and others, most of this opposition nowadays is confined to mortgage bankers or editors of ladies' magazines. At the Paris exhibition the hatred for Corbu's pavilion was passionate and vitriolic; indeed, it is difficult to understand why he was asked to participate in the first place, as the authorities did everything possible to sabotage his efforts. They began by giving him the worst site in the entire exhibition, a spot practically outside the exhibition grounds. Next, they erected a fence some eighteen feet high all around Corbu's pavilion to keep out visitors altogether. It took the intervention of a cabinet minister to have the fence torn down! Finally, when an international jury decided to award the first prize to Corbu's pavilion, the French member of the jury succeeded in vetoing the proposal on the grounds that the structure 'contained no architecture'.

Corbu has often been criticized for his lack of tact and his belligerence, but he has usually had just cause; virtually every single building put up or proposed by him in the 1920s and 1930s was treated with the same sort of contempt by the critics of the moment. As a matter of fact, it would be very difficult to find anyone who remembers another exhibit at the 1925 exhibition; only Corbu's pavilion has really survived the test of time.

It has survived that acid test not only because it was the first, clear statement of his notion of the 'superimposed villa', but also because it contained two further contributions for which the modern movement is indebted to Le Corbusier: first, a collection of exceedingly handsome modern furniture, some of it designed by him; and, second, a proposal for the reconstruction of the centre of Paris, which advanced Le Corbusier's city-planning ideas still further.

The committee that ran the Decorative Arts exhibition does, perhaps deserve some sympathy for its opposition to Le Corbusier's proposals. For Corbu made no secret whatever of his own contempt for 'decorative arts' as such: he believed 'that the sphere of architecture

51

embraces every detail of household furnishing, the street as well as the house, and a wider world still beyond both. My intention,' he explained, 'is to illustrate how, by virtue of . . . standardization . . . industry creates pure forms, and to stress the intrinsic value of this pure form of art that is the result.' Proceeding on this premise, Corbu furnished his pavilion with chromium-plated, tubular-steel furniture until then seen only in offices, and with standardized unit furniture (now generally referred to in America as 'storage walls') also very similar to utilitarian office furniture. In addition to these pieces, which Corbu redesigned to fit his own needs and taste, he used some of the most beautiful bentwood chairs produced before or since: the circular Thonet dining-chairs of bent 'sticks' of wood. The chairs had been designed during the Art Nouveau era of the late nineteenth century, and had been mass-produced ever since by their Austrian designer-manufacturer. Corbu, with his unfailing, selective eye, rediscovered them and made them famous again all over the world. As a direct result of Le Corbusier's rediscovery of the Thonet line of bentwood furniture, these nineteenth-century pieces are now treated as precious antiques and incorporated in the permanent collections of such institutions as New York's Museum of Modern Art. Indeed, the pressure for the revival of some of the designs has been so heavy that several manufacturers, including Thonet, have recently gone back to making one or two early chairs!

More will be said about Le Corbusier's furniture design in a moment; meanwhile, this exhibition pavilion, with its collection of 'useful objects', as well as examples of Cubist and post-Cubist painting and sculpture, was a convincing statement of the *aesthetic* position of the Machine Art men. Again, as on previous occasions, Corbu confused the issues by talking about 'practical machines for living in'. But by this time, with paintings by Léger and sculpture by Lipchitz displayed in his pavilion, no one had any excuse for failing to understand that Corbu was talking about a new world of *form*, rather than a new world of function.

The Plan Voisin [10] for the centre of Paris was exhibited in an annexe to the two-storey pavilion proper. It was an application of his Ville Contemporaine principles to an area of Paris roughly to the north-east of the Louvre. It is curious how close in spirit this radical plan was to the Tuileries and the Invalides!

Next to Corbu's pavilion in 1925, his most important small-scale experiments were five houses done between 1926 and 1929: the Cook

10. Portion of Plan Voisin for Paris, 1925. This model was exhibited in the Pavillon de l'Esprit Nouveau. (Courtesy, Museum of Modern Art)

house in Boulogne-sur-Seine (1926); the Villa Stein at Garches (1927); the two structures, also in 1927, for the Weissenhof exhibition in Stuttgart; and the Villa Savoye, at Poissy-sur-Seine, designed in 1929 and completed two years later. Several other buildings were done by Le Corbusier and Pierre Jeanneret during this period, but these five stand out in retrospect.

The Cook house [11] was a terrace house about twenty-five feet wide, an almost perfect prototype for a small, single-family urban dwelling using several of Le Corbusier's pet planning ideas. For example, the ground floor was almost entirely open; all it contained was a parking-space for a car, a small enclosed entry and stair hall, and a paved and planted open terrace. The upper floors were supported on a very few concrete *pilotis*. The second floor contained all the bed-rooms and baths, and the third and fourth floors contained all living areas.

As at Citrohan, Corbu made the most of the living areas upstairs by extending the living-room proper upward through two storeys, and by using a portion of the roof as a spacious garden terrace. But the most interesting fact about the Cook house was the extremely free handling of partitions: on every floor level Corbu made a point of curving his partitions to make it quite clear that they were entirely independent of all structural supports, and could be bent into any shape that might be

11. *Cook house, 1926. Prototype for a terrace house on stilts, with parking space below and roof patio above. (Courtesy, Museum of Modern Art)*

required by function or composition. (One of Corbu's favourite tricks was to enclose his lozenge-shaped bathtubs within form-fitting walls, and to suggest a possible location for a grand piano by bending one living-room wall into the shape of an elongated S. Some of his imitators later borrowed the shapes created by Corbu, and applied them indiscriminately to almost any interior and exterior element that could be bent out of shape without too much trouble. (A nice example of this sort of nonsense is the curved entrance canopy at New York's Museum of Modern Art. Unless its designers planned to use this canopy to support a grand piano and to conduct recitals on West Fifty-third Street, there does not seem to be much justification for its shape.) In any event, the Cook house was a forerunner of Corbu's later exercises in a sort of controlled plasticity – a direction that occupied him more and more in the years after the Second World War.

Even more convincing than the Cook house was the Villa Stein [12] (for Gertrude's brother), which he built at Garches during the follow-

12. Villa Stein, 1927. Another unit designed much like one of the 'super-imposed villas' of 1922. The house has a two-story-high 'hollow cube' and a roof garden. (Courtesy Museum of Modern Art)

ing year. Again: *pilotis* supporting a part of the ground floor; a hollowed-out, two-storey *outdoor* cube; freely curved partitions on every floor; a 'Golden Section' system of façade design; and a handsome sculptured roof garden on top [13]. The villa, in short, is another contribution towards Le Corbusier's central objective – to create prototypes for a vertical city.

The villa at Garches – recently restored though also, unhappily, altered – is so full of details that have influenced architects all over the world that it is difficult to list them all. Among them are the eloquently sculptured stairs and suspended entrance canopies, the long, uninterrupted ribbon windows, the interplay of levels and of forms. But Garches has another characteristic that has become a trademark of certain kinds of modern architecture: both its short end walls are blank, or almost blank. For Garches was designed again as a unit in a repetitive block of 'superimposed villas', and built on a rather narrow site. (In the Cook house the end walls were blank, too,

13. Roof garden of Villa Stein. (Courtesy, Museum of Modern Art)

for the simple reason that they were party walls in a strip of terrace houses.)

In all likelihood, the device of leaving the short end walls of his buildings blank grew out of Corbu's conviction that he was designing and building 'vertical slices' of some bigger unit, rather than independent houses in the landscape. Soon, however, the short, blank end walls became a kind of mannerism in much of his work, and only in very recent buildings has he opened up the short ends of his slab-like buildings, as well as the long façades. Actually, the contrast between a long, open, and glassy façade and a short, blank end façade turned out to be a very satisfactory aesthetic solution – especially in Corbu's Swiss Pavilion, built in 1932. But the origins of the idea, undoubtedly, are in Corbu's feeling that he was building units of a bigger whole, rather than complete, independent entities.

Perhaps the most sharply defined statements by Le Corbusier during these years are contained in the two houses [14] he built at the

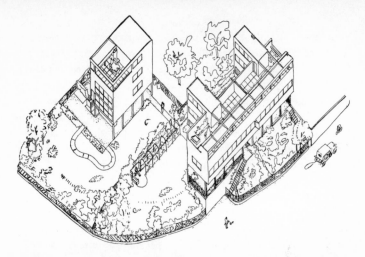

14. Bird's-eye view of the two units built at the Weissenhof exhibition, 1927. The house on the left is a typical Citrohan unit first designed in 1922; it is on stilts and has a roof patio. The building at right is an apartment house, also on stilts and with a roof garden. (From Œuvre complète)

Weissenhof exhibition in Stuttgart, also in 1927. He and a dozen other leading modernists from all over Europe had been invited by the exhibition's director, Mies van der Rohe, to contribute an experimental building to this modern suburb. Le Corbusier and Pierre Jeanneret were asked to design two. As the sponsors of the exhibition, the Werkbund (for which Gropius had designed his famous glass-faced administration building in 1914), believed strongly in the integration of art and modern industry, Corbu felt fully justified in making his Weissenhof buildings a kind of summary of all his convictions concerning an industrialized architecture.

Characteristically, he began with a statement of several hundred well-chosen words; and, just as characteristically, he started that statement with a highly self-conscious, chip-on-the-shoulder defence of his own position as an architect. 'This is by no means an aesthetic fantasy or a search for fashionable effects,' he informed his potential critics with ill-concealed contempt. 'We are dealing with architectural facts which call for an absolutely new way of building.' He then listed these facts, in this order: first, the *pilotis*, designed to raise the building off the ground and thus free the site and permit the garden to continue under and through the building; second, the *roof garden*, which, Corbu pointed out, meant in effect that all the ground covered by the buildings in a city could be recaptured in terms of parks up in the sky; third, the *open plan*, the result of a structural system of a very few widely spaced columns that permitted the utmost freedom in the arrangement of partitions and other space divisions; fourth, the *ribbon window* extending from one structural column all the way over to the next one, and thus allowing for uniform day lighting inside the building – unlike the traditional window (a hole punched into a structural wall), which, according to Corbu, creates pockets of gloomy darkness inside, next to rectangles of glaring light. And, finally, the *free façade*, as Corbu called it, by which he meant exterior walls that were no longer load-bearing and could, as a result, be opened up or closed at will, to satisfy functional or aesthetic require-ments. And he concluded: 'The above five basic points add up to a fundamentally new aesthetic. *Nothing remains for us of the architec-*

15. Apartment house at Weissenhof exhibition. Smooth and flat finish of façades is typical of Le Corbusier's work of this period. (Courtesy, Museum of Modern Art)

ture of earlier epochs . . .' Great men should certainly be permitted their quota of silly remarks, and Corbu – whose quota has been astonishingly small – was to reverse himself on this one in very short order.

The first of Le Corbusier's and Pierre Jeanneret's Weissenhof buildings was a precise and beautifully proportioned version of Corbu's Citrohan project of 1922: a white cube on stilts, with a two-to-one apartment on the second and third floors, and a clearly defined roof garden on top. Again the 'house' was really a slice of a city; but even when looked upon as a single, free-standing villa, the building had tremendous elegance. The free façade was treated somewhat like an abstract painting, with large rectangles of glass, vertical slot windows, and a single, boldly projecting balcony composed in the manner of a post-Mondrian painting.

The second building was an actual apartment house – or, rather, a portion of what we might call a garden-apartment unit [15]. Again on stilts, the building had single-level apartments on the second floor, and a roof garden on top. The stair towers were treated as separate elements, projecting out from the 'pure prism' of the apartment block. A ribbon of glass consisting of horizontally sliding windows of a design pioneered by Corbu extended across the full length of the building. All partitions inside consisted of prefabricated storage walls, and all furniture, other than chairs and an occasional table, was built in also. While this may seem fairly routine today, it was anything but routine in 1927. Corbu's built-in cabinets were so handsome that few furniture designers of the past thirty years have been able to improve on their proportions and details.

The Weissenhof buildings, in a sense, concluded one particular phase in Corbu's work. With their construction, he had in effect solved the problem of the vertical city building to his own satisfaction. While he has since gone far beyond Weissenhof in other city structures, his advances have been primarily aesthetic; the practical problem he had set himself was solved by 1927. His next and, possibly, his most important house, the Villa Savoye, revealed Corbu not only as a rational analyst of modern urban life, but as an architect in the finest traditions of the Western world.

NINE

Poissy-sur-Seine is a small town about an hour's ride from Paris. The Villa Savoye [16], in turn, is located in the centre of an estate of about a dozen acres, up in the hills overlooking Poissy and the valley of the Seine. Today the somewhat forbidding walls that surround the estate have begun to crumble, and the single gate, with the inevitable sign warning of a *chien méchant*, has rusted. No sightseers may enter the estate: Mme Savoye's instructions on that point are quite specific.

16. Villa Savoye, 1929–30. Entrance hall and garage are at ground floor; living areas and patio are on upper level; and a penthouse structure forms the roof. (Courtesy, Museum of Modern Art)

As a matter of fact, there is nothing very secret or private behind these walls. It is just that the owner would rather not have people see what is left of the house she was forced to abandon at the time of the German invasion, in 1940. For the famous Villa Savoye that Corbu designed in 1929 – one of the two or three most famous houses built anywhere in the past hundred years – is now a strange and rather tragic ruin.

Like all of Corbu's work, the Villa Savoye was not an isolated event in his creative life. It is part and parcel of the central concept he first developed in the Citrohan house in 1922 and brought to full flower in the apartment structure in Marseille exactly thirty years later. More specifically, the Villa was not even designed for the Savoye family or for that particular site: as early as 1925 Corbu had produced a poetic version of his favourite trinity – the stilt, the cube, and the sculptured roof [17] – for the Villa Meyer to be built near Paris, a project that was

17. *Roof structure of Villa Savoye. Patio and living-room are visible at lower left.* (*Courtesy, Museum of Modern Art*)

never realized except in a set of charming drawings. But regardless of the historical origins of the Villa Savoye, *it* – at least – was built; and *it* – rather than its predecessors – influenced perhaps half the modern houses built anywhere in the world during the past twenty-five or thirty years.

The Villa Savoye was the most complete, the most self-assured, the most convincing statement of Corbu's beliefs that he was able to produce in concrete and glass before he stopped being a young radical and started being a 'mature master'. Indeed, it might be said that most of his completed work before 1929 could, theoretically, have been built by other talented men of the younger generation. But the Villa Savoye could have been built only by a master.

What remains of the Villa Savoye today is, briefly, this: a streaky, grey, rectangular box of reinforced concrete, measuring about sixty feet square, raised up in the air and supported on a dozen round concrete *pilotis*. Deeply recessed under this concrete box, where the entrance foyer and garage used to be, there is now a hideously ugly pile of junk that looks, more or less, like the local village dump. Among the items in this junk pile, there are two old easy chairs of rattan; a coiled-up garden hose; several broken crates; an ancient Citroën sedan converted, at one time in its life, into a vegetable delivery truck; the remains of an old dining-table; and, depending upon the season of the year, a few dozen bales of hay. From inside this junk pile there emerge occasional muffled sounds; these suggest that the once elegant foyer of the Villa Savoye now serves as a stable for an asthmatic horse.

Upstairs, inside the great concrete box, things are not very different; most of the windows are boarded up; much of the floor area serves as a hayloft. The living-room contains an old workbench and a dilapidated tea-serving cart. A single, torn U.S. army-issue boot stands on the mantelpiece. Most of the paint has flaked off the walls; white splotches of plaster have appeared next to the original pastel blue. The patio, in the centre of this upper floor, is part hayloft, part weed garden.

Finally, the roof structure, one flight farther up by a long ramp: this is a composition of straight and curved concrete screens and forms, now as pale and flat and desolate as the rest – flaking paint, streaked concrete, rusty railings, weeds everywhere.

19. Still life painted by Le Corbusier in 1920. Geometric forms are similar to those found in elements of the Villa Savoye. (Courtesy, Museum of Modern Art)

Suddenly, out of a grey sky, there may flash a brief hint of the sun, and the ruin comes to life. The weeds become flowers, the flaking paint becomes an abstract mural, the great concrete shapes become plastic again, the few remaining walls of glass shine in the light. The Villa Savoye is as beautiful as it was in 1931, when Corbu completed it.

At Poissy, Le Corbusier made a series of fundamental declarations about architecture as he saw it: for example, he declared that he was a classicist about form and a classicist about nature. The Villa Savoye is divorced from the ground and raised up against the sky in a precise, geometric silhouette – raised up as if by some giant hand. (It is fascinating to see this recurrent theme of the giant hand raised against the sky in Corbu's sculpture from that time on: for example, the great symbol of his civic centre at Chandigarh, in India, some thirty years later, was a huge hand sculptured in wood and iron, held up to the winds!) The precise, geometric silhouette of the Villa Savoye permitted no confusion of architecture with nature. This was meant to be a man-made object, the product of man's one great distinguishing characteristic – pure reason. Frank Lloyd Wright, of course, would never, under any circumstances, have divorced a house from its natural setting. His houses don't just grow out of the land; they are *part* of the land, part of the mysticism that has always governed northern man's relationship to nature. They hark back to the mounds that conceal the ancient graves of Vikings, to Harlech Castle growing out of a Welsh hilltop, to Mont Saint-Michel; whereas Corbu's pure prism is the symbol of Mediterranean man's conquest of nature – the determination of sophisticated builders to shape their own habitat.

Corbu made this point even more clearly in another project built while the Villa Savoye was under construction. This was the penthouse apartment for Charles de Beistegui, on the Champs-Élysées [20]. Here, as in Perret's first apartment tower, the 'natural environment' consisted of neatly clipped boxwood hedges in classic, geometric forms and carefully planted in rectangular boxes so placed as to enclose the roof terraces and screen them against the Paris skyline. Should M. de Beistegui wish to take a quick look at that skyline – well, then, all he had to do was push a button and one entire section of boxwood hedge would disappear on an electric elevator. 'The complicated electrical installations required in this apartment,' Corby remarked at the time (and, presumably, with a straight face), 'required 4,000 metres of cable.' It is not likely that Frank Lloyd Wright would ever have put a plant on an elevator platform, to have it pop up or down at will, and it is perhaps even less likely that *anyone* except a

20. Penthouse for M. de Beistegui, 1930–1. The hedges that form the roof parapet were set on elevators and could be made to drop out of sight. (Courtesy, Museum of Modern Art)

Frenchman in love with modern machinery would ever describe a landscaping project in terms of the length of electric cable required to make it function.

At Poissy, a country house, the manipulation of nature is not nearly so mechanized, though it is no less sophisticated. The second-floor patio, upon which all living-spaces are centred, is the real garden: a paved courtyard with carefully controlled planting in boxes. Moreover, the views of the surrounding fields and trees are just as carefully controlled: on all four sides of the concrete box there are horizontal viewing slots through which sections of the landscape appear like naturalistic murals painted, between pilasters, in some great room of a Renaissance *palazzo*. Only the roof of this patio, this outdoor room, is entirely open – to the sky.

This, of course, is in the best tradition of Mediterranean building. Around the crowded basin of that sea, men have been forced for centuries to build vertically, and to enclose what they built with walls that could guarantee privacy from close-by neighbours. On the wide and spacious American prairie, where Wright grew up and learned to build with nature, men lived few and far between. They could build horizontally, parallel to the contours of the land, rather than up and away from them. The resulting differences were almost inevitable: as the Italian architect, Ernesto Rogers, has pointed out, Corbu's Mediterranean houses are patio houses, walled in, open only to the sky; Wright's prairie houses are like tents, with the walls rolled up. They are sheltered against the threatening sky with heavy, low-slung roof planes; and the visual limits of Wright's houses are those prairie horizons he learned to love in his youth.

The traditional Mediterranean separation of house and land lead Corbu into another conflict with Wright's philosophy. While Wright made a great point of using natural materials, preferably unfinished, to help him merge the house with its natural setting. Corbu gloried in making his building materials look as man-made as possible. The Villa Savoye was a reinforced-concrete structure finished smoothly and precisely with painted stucco. Its exteriors and interiors were largely white – the white that can look so plastic under a Mediterranean sky – but there were a few accents of colour on an occasional wall or partition. These colours came straight out of Corbu's painting: they were never the pure, primary colours of the bright and entirely flat sort used by Mondrian, but, rather, pastel shades that suggested three-dimensionality. Alfred Roth, the Swiss architect, pointed out some years ago that Le Corbusier's concept of colour was intimately related to his concept of space. Corbu's spaces are hollow cubes animated by contrasting geometric volumes like spiral stairs, cylindrical chimney flues, columns, and other objects of applied as well as fine art; these spaces are intensely plastic, vigorous, sculptural in the manner in which the white stucco houses on Greek islands like Mykonos are sculptural. And his sparing use of pastel shades, especially his pastel blues and charcoal greys, was designed to stress this plasticity of form. To a good many modern painters, the idea of making a flat, two-dimensional canvas look three-dimensional (or, for that matter, of making a flat wall look 'plastic') is sheer heresy; and when the De Stijl painters – Mondrian, van Doesburg, and others – wanted to be three-dimensional, they became sculptors. But Corbu was never bothered by such rationalizations, and his colour does what colour has been used to do from the beginning of time: it helps manipulate space and form.

There is another aspect to the finishes in the Villa Savoye and in Corbu's work prior to it which is worth mentioning. The Villa Savoye's exterior surfaces are a tautly stretched skin of stucco and glass, absolutely flush and finished as smoothly as Corbu knew how. The effect was that of a precise membrane stretched over a skeleton of concrete, and, indeed, inside the elevated patio the concrete skeleton is exposed and clearly differentiated from the outer membrane. This was a very popular façade treatment in Cubist and post-Cubist architecture, and it looked wonderfully machine-made – at least for the first month or so after the building was completed. Unfortunately, the weather started to take its toll before very long, and cracks and streaks appeared on the stucco surfaces. The harsh facts of practical building began to conflict with the intellectual concept. Frank Lloyd Wright, a country boy, always understood those facts and never failed to see a building in terms of time – to see how it would weather. But men like Corbu, who were and are city slickers at heart, went through some major disappointments before they were forced, in the end, to give up the flush stucco-and-glass membrane.

When they finally did give it up, some of the Machine Art men found themselves in real trouble because it became more and more difficult for them to produce buildings with sharply defined silhouettes. As soon as you begin to have roof overhangs, recessed panes of glass, projecting window sills, the silhouette of your 'pure prism' becomes considerably less pure and considerably less prism-like. So that today much of the Machine Art architecture that really works in terms of withstanding the test of time does not look very pure or simple.

Only Le Corbusier, and possibly Mies Van der Rohe, made the transition from the pure prism of buildings like the Villa Savoye to the three-dimensional façade without the slightest apparent difficulty. Corbu stuck to the taut membrane a little longer; but after the Second World War, when his work suddenly took on a rough and almost brutally virile cast, the taut membrane was discarded. In its place appeared a façade developed in depth, with receding voids and an occasional projection breaking up the (imaginary) surface of the prism, without ever really destroying its visual integrity. The basic, over-all form remained strong, simple, and geometric; indeed, it continued to look very plain and flat-sided from a distance. But at close quarters the pure prism became a many-faceted crystal, full of intriguing changes in light and shadow, colour and texture. If Corbu had built his Villa Savoye thirty years later, it would have been a 'rough', rather than a 'pure', prism.

That is one reason why the Villa has become one of the great historic monuments of modern architecture – one of its 'period pieces' – and why there was such a storm of protest when the building was threatened with destruction in 1959. In the spring of that year the town council of Poissy suddenly decided that the Savoye estate would make a fine site for a new high school; and plans were made to expropriate the estate, destroy the Villa and the little gate house, and erect a new school in their places. Almost within hours of the publication of this decision, André Malraux, De Gaulle's Minister for Cultural Affairs, found himself bombarded with letters, telegrams, and resolutions from architects all over the world demanding that the Villa be preserved. The question arose immediately – 'preserved for what?' In all likelihood it would cost tens of thousands of francs to restore the Villa, and Mme Savoye simply could not afford to spend such amounts. There were suggestions that the place be turned into a sort of retreat for young architects, in which they might continue their studies or, simply, continue their arguments. In any event, Malraux, who showed himself intensely conscious of the importance of Corbu's work, immediately intervened to save the buildings from further destruction. Whether or not a wealthy patron will be found to repair and endow the estate remains to be seen.

Meanwhile, as soon as the storm had subsided, the Villa returned to its lovely, surrealist dream existence – a delightful ruin, perhaps much better left that way. The war and the weather could destroy much of the original polish and sophistication of this building, but they could not destroy the great passion Corbu once poured into this little prism on stilts. Five years after the Villa Savoye was completed, he wrote this about architecture:

When the cathedrals were white . . . the new world was opening up like a flower among the ruins. Let us bring this joyful spectacle to life in our imaginations . . . and put clearly before our eyes those white cathedrals against the blue sky. We must get that image into our hearts . . .

When the Villa Savoye was white against the blue sky, it, too, was a 'joyful spectacle'. It is not that today. But the image remains in our hearts.

TEN

While the plans for the Villa Savoye were being drawn up, Corbu and Pierre Jeanneret were also at work remodelling an old house at Ville d'Avray, which was to contain the first group of chairs, tables, and cabinets completely designed by the architects. The year was 1928, and their collaborator on the interiors was Charlotte Perriand, one of the few great original furniture designers of recent times.

21. Interior at Ville d'Avray, 1928–9. All the furniture is by Le Corbusier and Charlotte Perriand. It includes the steel-and-leather version of the traditional 'British officer's chair', the form-fitting lounge-chair, and the heavily padded easy chair to the rear. All storage built in. (Courtesy, Museum of Modern Art)

The pieces at Ville d'Avray consisted of, among other things, three types of chairs which have spawned entire schools of furniture design since they first appeared [21]. There was, to begin with, a long, form-fitting reclining chair or lounge; next, a modern version of the traditional 'British officer's chair'; and, finally, a heavily upholstered easy chair. All three were framed in tubular steel either chromium-plated or enamelled, and the upholstery was of leather or black-and-white cowhide.

The reclining chair and the 'British officer's chair' were completely delightful and revealed much about Corbu's taste. Tubular-steel furniture, of course, was nothing very new: men like Marcel Breuer had designed tubular-steel chairs and tables at the Bauhaus in Weimar and Dessau from 1923 on, and Breuer's designs had been taken over by Thonet and other manufacturers to become almost standard items in most modern interiors. The quality that distinguished Corbu's designs from those of the Bauhaus was exactly the same that distinguished German functionalism from Corbu's rather special brand: while Breuer's chairs were entirely rational, technically impeccable, and, incidentally, very handsome, Corbu's were neither particularly rational, nor especially easy to manufacture. All they were, in fact, was ravishingly beautiful.

The reclining chair consisted of two entirely separate parts, an H-shaped cradle constructed, as Corbu remarked, *en tubes d'avion* (a characteristic reference to another technology: all it meant was that the tubes were oval in cross-section!). This cradle in turn supported a long, form-fitting, sled-shaped contraption of tubular steel and leather, whose angle could be freely adjusted. A good many designers have tried their hands at producing a simplified version of this chair, and a vulgar, massive copy of it is currently on the American market. Few of the copyists seemed to realize that the very complexity of this chair's structure was the ingredient that made it so wonderfully elegant.

This reclining chair and, to an even greater extent, the Corbu version of the smaller 'British officer's chair' [22] look like the complicated, beautifully articulated chassis of a Bugatti racing car. In the latter chair, for example, there are two chromium tubes that connect the front legs to the rear legs. In a Bauhaus chair these tubes would, quite obviously and soberly, have been straight. But in the Corbu chair the tubes start out straight and then, for no particular reason at all, suddenly leap up in a quarter-circle before they join the rear legs.

22. Easy chair by Le Corbusier and Charlotte Perriand, 1928. (Courtesy, Museum of Modern Art)

This and other little details – such as the cylindrical pillow strapped to the head of the reclining chair – make these just about the wittiest, sexiest chairs designed in modern times. The fact is, of course, that much modern steel furniture does tend to look a little grim; all of us who solemnly assert that we like it to do so because we think we *ought* to like it since it 'makes sense'. To a Frenchman this is a perfectly silly argument; he would never think of making love to a 'nice, sensible girl' as an Englishman might, or to a potentially 'good mother' as a German would. Corbu's chairs are rather like expensive tarts: elegant, funny, sexy, and not particularly sensible. Nobody has improved upon them to date.

The heavily upholstered easy chair was perhaps a little more practical: a rectilinear frame of tubular steel making a sort of square basket that, in turn, held squared-off leather pillows which formed the very comfortable seat. Eero Saarinen's easy chairs designed for the General Motors Technical Centre, and some recent pieces by the Danish architect Arne Jacobsen, are based on Corbu's development, but few other designers of the younger generation have tried to do anything further with this promising concept.

Corbu's dining and working tables of that year, however, have been copied by every furniture designer west of the Yangtze River. Basically there were two: a type with a recessed base of four legs joined by an H-shaped frame and made again of *tubes d'avion*; and another type with a square frame of angular, chromium-plated steel sections, with the legs at the corners of the table. The table tops were generally of glass to keep the furniture from obstructing visually the free flow of space; occasionally they might be of polished marble.

Corbu's chairs and tables are masterpieces of proportion and detail to any connoisseur, though they may look pretty much like a lot of other modern steel furniture to the layman. Apart from the conscious use of simple, geometric forms, such as prisms, cylinders, and cones, these chairs and tables reveal one other trademark of functionalism: the separation of functionally different parts of the same object. Corbu went to great lengths to differentiate in form and material between the thing you sit on in a chair, and the thing that does the hard work of supporting your weight (soft leather versus hard steel); the thing you work on in a table, and the thing that supports the table top (glass or marble versus *tubes d'avion*). This basic law of functionalism had been clearly established in Gropius's Bauhaus, but Corbu carried it even further – and, one suspects, sometimes with tongue in cheek. One of his dining tables, for example, has the standard H-frame for support plus the marble slab for the top; but nowhere does the slab touch the supporting frame. Instead, there are very thin pins of steel that grow out of the supporting frame and, in turn, support the table top.

These chairs and tables, together with some beautiful storage-wall units, were exhibited in 1929 in a modern apartment designed by

23. Model room designed for the Salon d'Automne, 1929. Free-standing and built-in furniture by Le Corbusier and Charlotte Perriand. (Courtesy, Museum of Modern Art)

Corbu, Jeanneret, and Charlotte Perriand for the Salon d'Automne [23]. The storage walls were particularly elegant, being framed in delicate sections of chromium-plated steel which formed a modular grid into which Corbu inserted units of shelving, storage drawers, glass-fronted display boxes, and mirrored sliding-door cabinets. The kitchen and bathroom designed as part of this apartment look as modern in almost every detail as the very latest built-in equipment being made by American manufacturers today. These same manufacturers and the industrial designers in their employ have spent years denouncing the 'angularity' and 'aridity' of Corbu's designs, only to come out with second-rate copies of the Salon d'Automne designs thirty years later (needless to say, without offering any financial reward to those who first conceived the ideas).

That many modern architects like Corbu, Breuer, Aalto, and Mies van der Rohe have devoted so much time to furniture design may be puzzling. The reasons are twofold: first, no modern architect believes that interior design can be separated from exterior design. The inside and the outside of a modern structure are regarded as one, thanks to the technological development of building with large sheets of glass, and the aesthetic development of sensing objects simultaneously from many vantage points. And, second, most modern architects have found chairs and tables to be excellent guinea pigs on which to experiment, simply and directly, with certain aesthetic and technical concepts. In a chair, for example, just as in a skyscraper, there are problems of function, of proportion, and of manufacture. Yet in a chair these problems can be studied much more readily (and economically) and their interaction observed much more readily than in a skyscraper. For this reason a piece of furniture has often taken the place of a small-scale sketch by means of which an architect was able to crystallize some new philosophic concept without going to any great expense.

With the exception of an occasional table or an occasional storage unit for a specific house, Corbu has not designed any furniture worth speaking of since 1929. Yet in this small group of chairs, tables, and cabinets, he produced a sufficient number of ideas, both of detail and of over-all form, to inspire a dozen or more furniture designers for many years to come.

By 1930, or thereabouts, Corbu had built only about a dozen relatively small villas, a housing development, and a couple of exhibition pavilions. He had also restored a river boat and turned it into a Salvation Army hostel, designed half a dozen pieces of furniture, written a similar number of books and propaganda tracts, and added a wing on stilts to another Salvation Army structure. In short, his architectural practice had been something less than a world-shaking success; yet his office was as busy as an ant heap, turning out projects and proposals for all sorts of buildings and new plans for cities. Many of his assistants were young European, Asian, and North and South American volunteers who had been drawn to Corbu's studio on the rue de Sèvres by his books and published projects. There was a spirit of tremendous excitement in his office at all times; yet the world outside continued to reject, denounce, and ridicule Corbu's ideas.

During the twenties an incident occurred which more than any other was to be responsible for Corbu's bitterness and coldness towards the world at large. Of course, he had already run into considerable trouble at the Exhibition of Decorative Arts, where his pavilion was surrounded by a gigantic fence to keep it out of sight; he had run into opposition at Pessac, where his housing units stood unoccupied for three years before local bureaucrats would issue the necessary occupancy permits; and almost every house built by him had run into criticism and violent attacks. But the hardest blow came to Corbu in 1927.

In that year an international competition was held for the design of the headquarters for the new League of Nations at Geneva. Le Corbusier and Pierre Jeanneret were among the 377 contestants, and their design was one of the few serious 'modern' projects submitted [24 and 25]. To a large segment of the international jury Corbu's proposal seemed outstanding: there was no question in their minds that it should receive first prize. Historians, with the admitted advantage of hindsight, agree with that view. However, politics, narrow-

24. *First project for the League of Nations Palace, 1927–8. The wedge-shaped auditorium was here developed for the first time.* (*Courtesy, Museum of Modern Art*)

25. *League of Nations Palace at pedestrian eye-level. Because the buildings are on stilts, there is an unobstructed view of Lake Geneva in the distance.* (*Courtesy, Museum of Modern Art*)

mindedness, and sheer stupidity triumphed, and a compromise was reached which was, in effect, no compromise at all, as it removed Corbu's project from all serious consideration.

The story is complex and has been reported in detail by Corbu's friend, the Swiss art historian Dr Sigfried Giedion. It is a pretty sordid story, of interest primarily because it tells something about the grim struggle Corbu and others had to wage before modern architecture became widely accepted.

Corbu's proposal for a site overlooking Lake Geneva consisted of four elements: a secretariat or office building for the day-to-day activities of the League; a large library; a wing containing meeting-rooms for various League of Nations commissions; and a great wedge-shaped Assembly Hall for the annual meetings of the foreign ministers. The four elements were extremely well integrated; the growing problems of automobile traffic had been clearly understood and met in a practical way; the symbolic requirements of the building had been solved by the use of impressive approaches to the main Assembly Hall, by the suggestion of sculpture in a grand, though entirely modern, manner, and by a massing of forms that clearly expressed the purpose of the buildings and their relationship to one another; the existing landscape had been respected as much as possible by the characteristic use of *pilotis*, which permitted the informal gardens to continue beneath and beyond most of the new structures; and the roof gardens proposed for the top of the Assembly Hall building formed a series of 'piazzas' with magnificent distant views across Lake Geneva. All these qualities were evident in Corbu's delicate and eloquent drawings for the project.

The importance of this design, however, went far beyond its inherent qualities. This was the first great challenge flung at the 'official' academicians by those who stood for the new architecture in Europe. It was an important event – the most important international design competition of the twentieth century. And though there were other modern submissions, only Corbu's represented an entirely serious, entirely practical proposal.

The jury consisted of six men: three 'modernists' – H. P. Berlage (Holland), Josef Hoffmann (Austria), Karl Moser (Switzerland); one Art Nouveau man – Baron Victor Horta (Belgium); and two traditionalists – Sir John Burnett (Great Britain), and M. Lemaresquier (France), a leading spirit of the Beaux Arts Academy, one of whose great contributions to the jury's sessions consisted of proving that

Corbu's drawings were rendered in printer's ink rather than Chinese ink – a serious violation of the programme! The three modernists settled on Corbu's proposal, and there was some hope that Horta might be willing to join them, as his own early work seemed to have much in common with the anti-eclectic approach of the modernists. After sixty-five jury meetings, however, Horta decided to vote with the traditionalists, and a tie resulted. The jury thereupon did two things: it decided to award nine first prizes, including one to Corbu; and it asked the political heads of the League to select from among the winners an architect who should get the actual job of building the League's headquarters. That left the problem just about where it had been before the start of the competition.

During the following two years, there was much public and private agitation about the character of the proposed structures. Corbu describes one typical incident in his own book of collected projects and buildings of the period.

A small paper, *La Suisse libérale* of Neuchâtel, published . . . in 1927 a series of articles by a Herr von Senger. These articles were put together in book form, published very quietly . . . and distributed gratis to munici-palities and federal offices, to create hostility to our endeavours at the exact moment when the final decision was about to be made on who was to build the Palace of the League of Nations. . . . What stuff for the journalists! Two years later, *Le Figaro*, in Paris, ran a series of articles from the talented pen of Camille Mauclair, with a sharpness bordering on the ridiculous. The attacks were based on the 'heroic' pieces that had appeared in 1927 in the 'heroic' *La Suisse libérale*. . . . And finally, in 1933, there appears a book by Camille Mauclair, entitled *L'Architecture, va-t-elle mourir?* . . . Mauclair certainly needs to be consoled: Camille, have you lost your head? . . . Architecture is far from dying, it enjoys the best of health. The new architecture is just being born!

No degree of sarcasm could gloss over the bitterness Corbu felt about the result of the League of Nations competition. The politicians had decided to select four traditionalists from among the nine win-ners; these four spent two years trying to arrive at a solution for the building complex. During those two years the site for the headquarters was changed, and Corbu and Jeanneret submitted a second design, even more open in its organization than the first, to fit the new site, When the League officials finally accepted the design agreed upon by the four traditionalists, the world (of architecture, at least) discovered to its amazement that the over-all plan proposed by the four men was remarkably similar to that suggested by Corbu, and entirely different in spirit and in detail from the designs originally submitted by the traditionalists in 1927. (The style, of course, was neo-classical.) Corbu and Jeanneret thereupon instructed their attorney to submit a detailed thirty-six-page brief to the League of Nations indicating that they felt their design had been pirated. The sole acknowledgement of this brief on the part of the League was a five-line letter stating that the organization could not concern itself with complaints submitted by individuals.

A dozen years later the original competition drawings by Le Corbusier and Pierre Jeanneret were purchased by the University of Zürich, and the bird's eye view of the project now hangs near the University's Department of Mathematics. Not far away, on the shores of Lake Geneva, stands the empty neo-classic palace that was actually built to house the League. It proved to be inadequate from the day it was finally opened, in 1937.

The League of Nations fiasco was only one of several major dis-appointments Corbu had to suffer in the late twenties and early thirties. The blows came with the monotonous regularity of a twenty-one-gun salute. There was, for example, the rejection of Corbu's proposal for a new Palace of the Soviets, in 1931; there were the city plans for Algiers from 1930 to 1934, with their fluid forms and their mile-long curvilinear buildings; and there were the plans for Paris, for Antwerp, for Stockholm, and for many other large cities – all painstakingly worked out in great detail, all rejected, sometimes by juries after competitions, at other times by local authorities without benefit of jury advice.

To say that all this work was in vain is obviously not true. Through-out the world younger (and more tactful) architects avidly studied every line drawn and published by Corbu, and began to 'sell' the ideas to more receptive clients. To Corbu there was, perhaps, some sense of satisfaction in seeing his ideas so widely accepted elsewhere; but he would have been less than human if he had not grown increasingly bitter at seeing his work copied without any benefit whatever to himself.

For the record, it is perhaps worth listing some of Corbu's brilliant innovations of these years. Many of these innovations finally bore fruit in the hands of young architects, who have never denied their debt to Le Corbusier, and who have made it clear that Corbu devel-oped certain solutions that simply cannot be improved upon at the moment. Such men as Eero Saarinen, who died in 1961, and who regarded Corbu as one of the great 'form givers' of modern archi-tecture, would have been the last to deny that he was enormously influenced by the forms Corbu gave to modern architecture. The same holds true of Corbu's Brazilian disciple, Oscar Niemeyer, whose work would be completely unthinkable without Le Corbusier's tutelage; and of the late, brilliant, Polish-born architect Matthew Novicki, killed in 1950 in an aeroplane crash in the Egyptian desert,

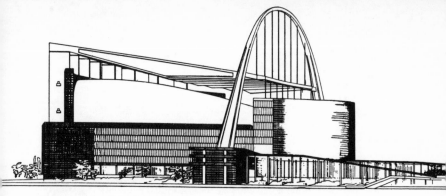

26. Project for the Palace of the Soviets, 1931. Part of the great assembly hall at left was to have been suspended from the parabolic arch. (From Œuvre complète)

who had received his apprenticeship in Corbu's studio in Paris before the Second World War. These men Le Corbusier accepts as worthy followers; and though he can hardly be blamed for wishing that he had had some of the opportunities available to the generation that followed him, he recognizes the hardships of his life as part of the price you must pay for being the first.

For Corbu was first with an astonishing number of ideas that seem startling even today when imitated by his many admirers: the huge parabolic arch from which was hung the roof of the Great Hall of the Palace of the Soviets [26], for example, was a brilliant piece of structural exhibitionism, scaled to the monumental occasion. Here was to be an assembly hall for 15,000 spectators and 1,500 'performers' – a fantastic political circus. And Corbu developed a scheme that was a spectacle in itself, yet so carefully thought through in terms of human progression on different levels and by different means that somehow an understandable scale was preserved. Since that competition (to which Corbu had been invited by Soviet authorities as a sop to Western 'progressives' disappointed by the League of Nations fiasco), the great parabolic arch has fascinated many other architects: Saarinen used the device for his prizewinning Jefferson Memorial design for St Louis (now being built), and Mussolini had a much smaller parabolic arch built for himself as a war memorial to celebrate his dreams of empire. Corbu's design, however, did not get off the paper it was drawn on. 'Out of considerations which I must recognize,' he stated, 'the jury of this competition decided that

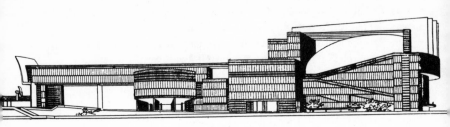

the Palace of the Soviets should be built in the Italian Renaissance style. It must be admitted,' he added, almost audibly gnashing his teeth, 'that a Palace which in form as well as technique should be an expression of the new age, can only be the result of a social development that has reached a high point – and not of one at the beginning.'

In 1933, two years after the Soviet Palace, Corbu entered another competition – this one for the headquarters building of a life-insurance company, to be erected in Zürich. He explained that the programme, as written for that competition, simply did not take cognizance of the possibilities offered by new techniques in planning and construction; hence he ignored the programme (which had envisaged a low structure with a central court) and produced a ten-storey office building whose organization in terms of structure, heating, air-conditioning, functional relationships, and so on was explained in his drawings in the most meticulous way possible. The result of that competition for Corbu and his cousin Jeanneret was just as expected: their entry was immediately disqualified, as it did not satisfy the traditional preconceptions held by the client. Yet here again Corbu presented a series of ideas that have come to life in other buildings by other architects in the years since the Rentenanstalt project was first presented. For example, here was the first office tower with a lozenge-shaped plan, the shape having been arrived at by the simple rationalization that the elevator core in the centre of a slablike building required extra space, and that such a slab should, therefore, be fattened up in the middle. Today at least three such lozenge-shaped towers have been built: the B. C. Electric building in Vancouver, completed in 1956; the Pirelli building in

Milan, completed in 1959; and the Pan-Am tower near Grand Central Station in New York, first projected in that same year. Like the Salvation Army hostel in Paris, built in 1932–3, the Rentenanstalt was to have been sheathed in glass and equipped with window-washing platforms suspended from trolleys on the roof – a standard American practice today. And, like so many of today's most distinguished tall buildings, the Rentenanstalt was to have a penthouse of curved and vaulted planes, housing (among other things) a theatre.

The various projects for the rebuilding of Algiers (all of them bogged down in a bureaucratic morass) represent modern solutions to the typical crowded Mediterranean town which had first introduced Corbu to certain concepts of architecture – especially to the image of the white-walled patio open to the brilliant blue sky. Somehow the plastic coastline of Algiers, covered with clusters of walled buildings, kept Corbu intrigued for many years; and in responding to its landscape and townscape, Corbu created some of his most brilliant projects for terrace houses, terraced apartments, and multi-level highways that effectively sorted out different kinds of traffic and made them work together and separately. One of his most interesting solutions for Algiers was a tall hillside apartment house, designed to be built in continuous strips, and entered on the uphill side on a floor half-way up the building. This entrance floor was to be open, so that pedestrians on the uphill side of the building could enjoy a continuous view of the Mediterranean, framed between horizontal slabs of concrete. At this entrance level and just below it, there was to be a continuous highway and parking space. With characteristic thoroughness, and with his characteristically French delight in the complexities of machinery, Corbu even laid out the ducts for an air-conditioning system, although his building was designed as a complete breeze-way, with apartments extending right through the structure from north to south. (This principle has become common practice in all tropical hotels built since the end of Second World War.) Towards the north and the view of the Mediterranean, Corbu placed his double-storey living areas. But the most intriguing aspect of the Algiers project was the fact that the buildings, in effect, became continuous highways – a concept now being revived in many parts of the world.

The city plan for Antwerp, produced in 1933 as a competition entry, fared no better than Corbu's other projects. 'Crazy stuff', the jury called it, and passed on to more 'practical' submissions. Yet the

Antwerp plan does not look very different today from such eminently sound proposals as those made by the architect Victor Gruen for Fort Worth: the creation of a largely pedestrian city core ringed by super-highways. Even more impressive in terms of today's best city-planning practice is Corbu's proposal for Stockholm, also done in 1933; here, at least, the jury paid Corbu the compliment of studying his proposals for all of ten months – only to reject them in the end. Yet there is literally nothing in these proposals which would not seem entirely reasonable today to the city-planning commissions of Philadelphia, New Haven, Chicago, Los Angeles, or Cleveland. In fact, Corbu may, if anything, have *under*estimated the problems raised by interlocking automobile and pedestrian traffic; today's American planners would probably feel that the separation should be even more complete than Corbu suggested in the early thirties.

'The defeats of these past years represent so many victories,' Corbu said in 1934. 'Our rejected plans will become public accusers, for the public will judge the bureaucrats according to these plans; and the day will come when these plans will force a change.' To many of his contemporaries, Corbu may have seemed to be whistling in the dark; but his faith was real enough – a Frenchman's passionate faith in the eventual triumph of reason.

THIRTEEN

Despite the disappointing outcome of the League of Nations competition and of many of his other projects, the furore they created helped advance the cause of modern architecture in general and Corbu's career in particular. In the summer of 1928 Corbu, Giedion, and other leading architects of the modern movement banded together to form CIAM (Congrès International d'Architecture Moderne). One of the prime movers of CIAM in its early days was Mme de Mandrot de la Sarraz; she offered her family's old Château de la Sarraz for the first meeting of the group and helped it in numerous other ways. (Incidentally, she also commissioned Corbu to design a house for her a couple of years later.) At this first CIAM meeting, Corbu outlined a programme for discussion which ranged from subjects like 'modern technology and its consequences' to 'city planning' and 'the education of young architects'. CIAM was to become a powerful force in the modern movement, and its influence can be felt to this day, particularly through certain schools of architecture. In 1928, however, it was in effect a sort of defensive alliance of architects and planners who believed that the League of Nations competition and other fiascos required them to stick together and form their own pressure group.

Even though Corbu lost the League of Nations job, he was soon busy designing his first large structures: the Centrosoyus for Moscow (1928), headquarters for the Soviet Cooperative Unions, and now the Soviet Ministry for Light Industry; a multi-storey apartment building for Geneva (1930–2); a smaller one in Boulogne-sur-Seine with an apartment for the architect on top (1932); a large Salvation Army hostel in Paris (1932–3); and the Swiss Pavilion – a student dormitory building – in the University City in the south of Paris (1930–2).

Of these five buildings the Centrosoyus, a huge complex for some 2,800 office workers, is by far the largest. Apart from this, the Centrosoyus is interesting primarily because in it some of the concepts originally projected for the League of Nations were finally executed; and because its multi-level public areas, with their great, sweeping ramps, showed Corbu at his sculptural best. The structure was probably the last 'modern' building of any consequence erected in the U.S.S.R. before the party line swung to wedding-cake architecture. Although the Centrosoyus was built without Corbu's supervision, it was still the most modern and self-assured building in Moscow more than twenty-five years after its completion.

The Salvation Army hostel, whose glass façade was badly damaged during the Second World War (and even more badly repaired), was a fantastic piece of planning, with elaborate interior automobile and pedestrian ramps, a library, dining and sleeping facilities, etc., all contained within a narrow, slablike building on a rather complicated site. The air-tight glass façade, designed to simplify air-conditioning, could be washed by men standing on a platform that was suspended from a trolley travelling back and forth along the edge of the roof garden – a forerunner of a similar mechanism installed at New York's Lever House when it was built after the Second World War.

The Salvation Army hostel is much more glassy, much more metallic in detail than most of Corbu's buildings before or since. In addition to plate glass, Corbu sparingly used a glass block – one of the few instances in recorded history when that hideous material was used well. (One reason was that French glass block, unlike that produced in the United States, was small and rather handsomely patterned.) Although the Salvation Army building was full of elegant detail, it suggests, in retrospect, that Corbu is at his best when he stresses reinforced concrete in all its plastic possibilities.

The Swiss Pavilion [27], which was indeed supported on a reinforced-concrete substructure, is not as large as the Salvation Army hostel, or as complex in terms of planning. But in the history of modern architecture this little five-storey building is one of the most important 'vertical slabs' built before the Second World War, and it is one of the three or four most beautiful 'vertical slabs' built at any time during the past few decades.

This is so for several reasons: first, and most importantly, the Swiss Pavilion is a building of disarming simplicity and purity – a precise, four-storey vertical slab, free-standing and raised one storey above the ground on *pilotis*. Secondly, the Swiss Pavilion is a wonderfully effective play of contrasting forms: the pure prism of the steel-framed slab contrasted with the massively sculptured concrete *pilotis*; the

27. *Swiss Pavilion, University City, Paris, 1932. The first completely uncompromising slab building constructed by Le Corbusier. (Courtesy, Museum of Modern Art)*

smooth and slightly curved shaft of the stair tower contrasted with the free-formed ground-floor structure that contains the entrance foyer, the communal lounge, and the janitor's apartment [28]. Third, the Swiss Pavilion is full of striking surface contrasts: the curved rubble-stone wall on the ground floor as opposed to the smooth stone-veneer finish on the building proper; the all-glass south façade along three floors as opposed to the stone-veneer finish on the high parapet of the roof patio (the parapet, in turn, being punctured here and there to create the same sort of 'viewing slots' Corbu used in the patio of the Villa Savoye); and, similarly, the contrast between the open façade

28. Rear of the Swiss Pavilion, showing curved stair tower and the stone-faced communal areas at ground level. The natural stone wall was set into a concrete frame and treated much like a mosaic. (Courtesy, Museum of Modern Art)

to the south, the blank façades facing east and west, and the punctured façade facing north. Finally, the Swiss Pavilion is an exceptionally clear statement of the aesthetic of functionalism. Its three principal elements – the slab, the ground-floor structure, and the stair shaft – are all clearly articulated, separated, and then linked in a manner that emphasizes, rather than detracts from, their separateness.

During the war a German anti-aircraft unit mounted some 20-mm. Bofors guns on the roof of the Swiss Pavilion, and the recoil shook up the building here and there. However, there was no structural failure of any sort; the Pavilion was repaired at little cost, and by 1950 looked as good as new [29]. Le Corbusier painted a long floor-to-ceiling mural on to the inside of the curved rubble-stone wall in the student lounge, replacing a photo mural he had put there originally.

The Swiss Pavilion has been the forerunner to so many famous slab buildings that it is hard to mention them all. The most obvious one, of course, is the slab of the United Nations Headquarters, for which Corbu himself was one of the architectural consultants. Another is the Ministry of Education building in Rio, designed by Oscar Niemeyer in consultation with Le Corbusier, Lucio Costa, and others in 1936; and there are various and sundry postwar hotels, apartment buildings, and office towers built in the United States, South America, Europe, Asia, Africa, and Australia. All of these buildings have four things in common with Corbu's Swiss Pavilion: they are vertical slabs; they have long, glassy façades, and short, blank façades; they are raised on stilts; and the ground-floor space – whether it be a lobby, assembly hall, or shopping area – is treated as a free-form structure that is 'slid' under the raised slab and handled as a separate and contrasting element.

The Swiss Pavilion and one or two houses of the same period reveal another development of major significance in Corbu's work: the use of traditional, natural materials. Corbu's curved rubble-stone wall at the Swiss Pavilion is framed in concrete like an abstract mosaic. There is no intention of making the wall look 'natural': like all the rest of his architecture, the wall is meant to look sophisticated and man-made – in fact, rather painterly. The stone looks and is treated almost like a very rich sort of wallpaper, applied to the structure, but not trying to look as if it held up anything whatever.

The vacation house for Mme de Mandrot, built near Toulon while the Swiss Pavilion was under construction in Paris, was of local rubble stone also; but that is where any resemblance ends between it and the Pavilion – or, for that matter, between it and any of Corbu's earlier houses. For here Corbu suddenly began to experiment with something that must have shocked a good many of his Machine Art friends: he took a primitive, local building tradition and transformed it, with infinite sophistication, into an entirely modern statement.

Corbu's interest in traditional and natural materials was not as sudden as it may have appeared. Throughout his trips in south-east

Europe, Greece, Italy, and North Africa he had been struck by the virility of simple, native construction. As early as 1923, in *Vers une architecture*, he made references to primitive building. By the late twenties he had started to use an occasional wall of local stone to contrast with the precision of his white cubes. The charming little gate house for the Villa Savoye (a sort of 'baby' to the Villa proper) had a base of stone; Corbu's own apartment [30 and 31], in Boulogne-sur-Seine, has party walls of brick and concrete block – left unfinished (in his studio, at least) just as he found them on the site.

But the house for Mme de Mandrot and the later summer house at Mathes were built entirely, or almost entirely, with natural materials. They had bearing walls of native stone supporting floors and roof, with occasional inserts of glass and wood. The de Mandrot house still had reinforced-concrete elements (floor slabs and an occasional concrete column where the bearing wall had been replaced with a large expanse of glass); but the summer house at Mathes was all stone and wood, with massive wooden posts, beams, and planks next to equally massive walls of local stone.

As in the Swiss Pavilion, Corbu treated these natural materials in the most elaborately sophisticated way. The stone walls of the house for Mme de Mandrot are framed panels and look almost painted rather than real. On the inside they were whitewashed because, as Corbu observed a long time ago,'white is always powerful and positive'. No attempt whatever was made to 'merge' the house with the landscape; indeed, it stands on a small platform, built on a sort of promontory from which there is a beautiful view of a plain. Yet, despite its anti-naturalism, the house looks just 'right' in a formal French landscape.

The summer house at Mathas was built in 1935. It is two storeys high, has a 'butterfly roof' (V-shaped in cross section) and a simple, rectangular plan. Both floors have their circulation along an outside 'corridor' – a terrace and a balcony; the wooden structure is quite traditional in principle and clearly expressed. It is a house that explains itself without any trouble, inside and out.

These two houses, together with a couple of other projects of the same period [32], are the forerunners of many of the modern stone, wood, and glass houses we see all around us in the United States. Of course, Frank Lloyd Wright had used these materials in their natural state for many years, long before the house for Mme de Mandrot was built. But Wright used them in a naturalistic way – i.e., in a way that

30. Le Corbusier's own apartment, Paris, 1933. This two-storey unit occupies the top floors of a building designed by Le Corbusier. The apartment shows his increasing interest in more sculptural forms. (Courtesy, Museum of Modern Art)

31. Studio in Le Corbusier's apartment, showing paintings and sculpture of the 1930s. The rough brick and concrete blocks add texture to the space. (Courtesy, Museum of Modern Art)

32. Week-end house at Vaucresson, 1935. Traditional and natural materials are used sparingly but with growing frequency. (Courtesy, Museum of Modern Art)

was anathema to all believers in a machine aesthetic. Now Le Corbusier, the greatest Machine Art apostle of them all, had found a way of using traditional materials in an entirely modern, almost abstract manner. He had made natural materials respectable in terms of the Machine Art idiom.

As usual, Corbu developed innumerable details in these stone-and-wood houses that have inspired his admirers: in the stone-and-wood Errazuris house in Chile, designed in 1930, there is the first dramatic, modern use of the unequal butterfly roof, bridging a house that is part two storeys, part one storey in height. Ramps that connect the levels are parallel in slope to the pitch of the roof – a very handsome spatial organization, quite different from the more common butterfly roof used so often today without the slightest relationship to the interior. In the house at Mathes the fenestration is worked out as part of a panel system, part glass, part plywood, painted in brightly contrasting pastel colours – all inserted in a grid of wooden vertical and horizontal divisions. This idea, too, has been copied again and again ever since. In that same house there are post-and-beam connexions that have been more or less standard for centuries, but were never used in Machine Art architecture until Corbu rediscovered their beauty and strength.

However much Le Corbusier might shy away from naturalism in architecture, his rediscovery of natural materials brought with it a revival of interest in natural forms *per se*. In a letter to a group of young South African architects, dated 1936, Corbu wrote:

How are we to enrich our creative powers? Not by subscribing to architectural reviews, but by undertaking voyages of discovery into the inexhaustible domain of Nature! . . . I wish that architects would sometimes take up their pencils to draw a plant or a leaf – or to express the significance of the clouds, the ever-changing ebb and flow of waves at play upon the sands . . .

This, of course, is precisely what Frank Lloyd Wright had been saying to disciples at Taliesin for quite some time, between acid cracks at that 'pamphleteer and painter', Le Corbusier, who seemed to think that architecture was just a matter of piling boxes upon more boxes. Whether Corbu realized it or not, this rediscovery of the 'inexhaustible domain of Nature' was the beginning of a new phase entirely in his own work – a phase that, as time went on, he was to call 'organic'.

In the late autumn of 1935 Corbu made his first trip to the United
States. The Museum of Modern Art was arranging for an exhibition
of his work, and invited him to come to New York for a series of
lectures in connexion with that show.

New York struck Corbu like a bombshell – and vice versa. 'New
York, clothed in pearly haze and stretching its distant towers to the
sky, appeared before me in the morning mist like the promised city,'
Corbu said about his arrival. 'This was the land of modern times and
this was that fantastic and mystic city – the temple of the New World!'
Le Corbusier, the man who had designed the best skyscrapers and
skyscraper cities ever put on paper, had never seen a real skyscraper
before in his life! 'When I first saw the Empire State Building,' he told
a friend in India, several years later, 'I wanted to lie down on my back
right there on the sidewalk, and gaze towards its top for ever.' He was
completely stunned by the sheer size of the thing. 'A thousand feet
high!' he said. 'That is an event in the history of architecture!'

Yet Corbu was not entirely dazzled by New York, Chicago, or
Detroit. Granted, the technical skill that produced the skyscraper was
one thing; but the aesthetic ignorance that adorned it with massive
gimcrack was another. And still under consideration – the *most*
important consideration in Corbu's mind – was this: the fact that the
architects and planners of the United States had not the foggiest idea
of what to do with the skyscraper *as a tool of city planning*! With his
usual perceptiveness, Corbu pointed out that a skyscraper without a
city plan was sheer nonsense.

His trips around the United States in late 1935 and early 1936 were
peppered with speeches, interviews, and debates. To Corbu, this was
a stimulating time: at long last he was in the land of Machine Art and
in the land of the Ville Radieuse – the twin subjects that had fascinated him for years. But what was the reality? He told one successful
New York architect, while standing at the window of that man's office
and looking at Manhattan's skyline, that all those skyscrapers were a

disgrace to the engineering skill that produced them. 'And here I was,' his host complained later, 'with this man tearing down everything I had been doing all my life!' He told the New York *Herald* that 'New York's skyscrapers are too small', and the *Herald* made it an incredulous headline. He told a dazed New York police official, Harold Fowler, over a breakfast conference, that Manhattan would have to be rebuilt from the ground up. He told a Chicago audience, that 'as a result of indifference and the all-consuming power of money, irresponsible enterprise has been the controlling influence on [U.S.] town-planning . . . The great inefficiency of America,' he continued, 'has enabled me to see more clearly the nature and inevitable end of our present city development . . .'

In short, Corbu was not particularly tactful; unlike the stereotype of the 'European visitor on his first trip to the United States', Corbu was by no means starry- and dewy-eyed. He decided, quite simply, to tell the truth, and the truth turned out to be quite painful.

The most painful truth Corbu decided to tell had to do with the American skyscraper city and its chaotic approach to planning. In a letter addressed to Kenneth Stowell, then editor of the *American Architect*, Corbu gave one of the most brilliant analyses ever produced of what plagued the U.S. city – and what would plague it in days to come unless certain specific measures were taken immediately. This letter was written by Corbu in 1936, over a quarter of a century ago; if much of Corbu's criticism sounds familiar to us today, it has become so only because the highest American planning authorities, from the mayors of great cities down to New York's chief planners (who often like to deprecate those from whom they have acquired their wisdom), have now come to understand what Corbu saw so clearly in 1936.

The New York skyscraper is only negative [Corbu wrote]. It has destroyed the street and brought traffic to a standstill. It consumes the very life of the population and eats up whole districts around itself, emptying them and bringing ruin. Build the skyscraper bigger and more really useful, [place it in a park] and it will reclaim a vast amount of land, will compensate for depreciated properties, will provide a perfect system of circulation, and will bring trees and open spaces into the city. The pedestrians will have the freedom of parks over the whole ground area and the cars will travel from skyscraper to skyscraper at a hundred miles an hour on one-way elevated roads placed at wide distances apart . . . Notice how the great hotels and apartment houses [around Central Park] have naturally come to be built here so as to have the advantage of looking out on space. But Central Park is too big; it is an island in a sea of buildings. Crossing it is like traversing no-man's-land. The trees, grass and . . . space of Central Park ought to be multiplied and spread over the whole of Manhattan . . .

The suburb is the great problem of the U.S.A. . . . I give a lot of thought to those crowds who have to return by subway in the evening to a home which is anything but paradise. Those millions who are condemned to a life without hope, without a resting place . . . Manhattan [as it is now] is so antagonistic to the fundamental needs of the human heart that the one idea of everybody is to escape. To get out. To avoid wasting one's own life and that of one's family in that hard, implacable atmosphere. To see the sky. To live where there are trees and to look out on grass. To escape for ever from the noise and racket of the city.

Millions of city dwellers have moved out to the country. They arrive and settle down and in so doing they cause the destruction of the country. The result is a vast, sprawling built-up area encircling the city – the suburbs. All that remains is the dream . . .

This suburban development makes necessary the hours spent daily on subways, buses and commuter trains; it causes the destruction of that communal life which is the very marrow of the nation.

What Corbu predicted during his first American trip has now become a nightmare reality. Today's city planners in New York and elsewhere are trying, desperately and almost hopelessly, to create zoning patterns that will eventually force the kind of space distribution which, Le Corbusier realized, could still turn Manhattan or downtown Chicago into open cities punctuated with glistening skyscrapers, spaced far apart and linked by ribbons of expressways. Legislation passed by federal and state governments in recent years tries to achieve the same results – and tries to break through the stranglehold of thick belts of grim suburbia built since the Second World War. As so often happens, the poet has been vindicated, and his 'practical' and 'hardheaded' critics have been exposed for their lack of vision.

But shortsighted officials were not the only ones who failed to understand Corbu. The advocates of the horizontal 'Garden City' on the English pattern were vehement in their opposition to what they considered to be Corbu's 'inhuman' proposals. These planners of villages scaled to the demands of eighteenth- or nineteenth-century life believed – and some actually still believe – that the American city can be dissolved into low-density patterns of housing (i.e., detached, semi-detached, and terrace houses in garden settings) which will, somehow, be grouped in small satellite communities, each with its own self-supporting industry, commerce, and agriculture, each linked to its neighbour, far away, by highways criss-crossing the countryside. This naïve and romantic notion presupposes several things that simply do not correspond to the facts of modern life: first, it assumes that small-scale industries are economically practicable; second, it assumes that there is enough space in the U.S. to spread out the population horizontally (or, if this is not the assumption, then the Garden City planners evidently believe that either universal birth control or a revival of the bubonic plague will drastically reduce the overpopulation of the globe); and, third, it assumes that people don't like to live in big cities. This is simply not true.

Most people like big cities so much that they are willing to put up with them even though the big city has become virtually uninhabitable. This is clearly demonstrated by the increasing flight from the country into town and cities; only prejudice can obscure it. The problem today, obviously, is not to ship people out of New York, Chicago, Los Angeles, or St Louis and offer them wholesome living in village-like satellite communities; it is, quite simply, to create a new kind of city – a city with all the excitement, the stimulation, the glamour, the gregariousness of a big metropolis – and to make that city healthy, efficient, and beautiful.

The principal factors that make Le Corbusier a twentieth-century prophet and Frank Lloyd Wright a nineteenth-century romantic are in their different reactions to the city: Wright hated it, wanted to destroy it, hoped to dissolve it in a horizontal spread of greenery; Corbu loves the city, wants to make it more dramatic, more exciting, more efficient, and, above all, more beautiful. It was quite characteristic for Wright to design his few city buildings – like the Johnson Wax building in Racine, Wisconsin, and the Guggenheim Museum in Manhattan – to look like some foreign object, inexplicably dropped into the urban fabric, but, on the other hand, to design his many country buildings to merge and melt into their natural environment. And it is just as characteristic for Corbu to design his many city buildings to fit perfectly into the angularity of an urban pattern, and to make his few country buildings seem a little out of place in a natural setting. For to Corbu the city is the great challenge, the great contemporary problem. Regardless of whether one regrets this or not, the facts of the world's population statistics support Le Corbusier.

His American trip took Corbu to Detroit, where he saw the Ford assembly line – and immediately wrote an ode to it! Here was the America of Machine Art. Corbu wrote:

> When the cathedrals were white [i.e., when they were first built], everybody worked together in complete unison. In Ford's factory, every-one works to one end, all are in agreement, all have the same objective, and all their thoughts and actions flow along the same channel. In the building industry there is nothing but contradictions, hostility, pulling in opposite directions, differences of opinion, working at cross-purposes and marking time. We pay dearly for all this – to build is a luxury and, consequently, society is badly housed . . . Let the forces which up to now have been pulling in opposite directions mass themselves to march solidly together. . . . Let the ghosts of the past cease to bar the way.

Although Le Corbusier met with a great deal of enthusiasm among students and young architects wherever he went, his public reception, as exemplified by some newspapers and institutions, left something to be desired. Needless to say, certain papers that expect foreign visitors to go through the standard ritual of prostrating themselves before the miracle of America were not charmed by Corbu's acid criticism of the country whose guest he was. He was, of course, quite familiar with this sort of thing from his frequent bouts with the authorities and the press in Europe. What hurt him more were certain misunderstandings that arose during his visit, particularly a misunderstanding with the Museum of Modern Art, which had agreed to pay him a fee for a number of lectures. According to Corbu the fee was too small; more-over, he claimed, the agreement had committed the Museum's direct-ors to much more assistance than they seemed willing to give. Were not the Rockefellers 'behind' the Modern Museum? Was it not reasonable to expect them to pay adequately for a visit from the prophet?

Regardless of the merits of his case, Corbu had little to complain about regarding his treatment by the Museum of Modern Art. As early as 1932 Henry-Russell Hitchcock and Philip Johnson had put together an exhibition on 'International Architecture' which praised and exhibited Corbu's works as of the greatest importance to his time. (The term 'International Style' was coined on the occasion of this exhibition by the Museum's leading spirit, Alfred Barr.) And though the Museum *was* in part supported by the Rockefeller family, it had to pay most of its own way and simply did not possess the sort of funds a European, full of notions about American wealth, might expect. Corbu has had misunderstandings regarding money matters before and since: he feels, quite rightly, that very few of his ideas have ever paid him a financial return; that ideas are, however, the only commodity an intellectual can sell to pay the rent; and that, finally, he should be paid for presenting his ideas whenever possible, particularly as it would seem that others are much more likely than he to turn these ideas into cash. The argument is perfectly reasonable, although it is considered unorthodox in a society that thinks of its intellectuals as nearly worthless, and will pay 'idea men' best when their ideas can be made to produce or sell goods. Still, the Museum of Modern Art, a non-profit-making organization, can hardly be compared to a big advertising agency; and so Corbu's demands could not be fully met. This was the beginning of a feud between Corbu and America which rages to this day: first he denounced the Museum; then, by indirection, the Rockefellers; next, during the time of the building of the United Nations after the Second World War, Corbu became convinced that the Rockefellers were again behind some sort of plot to deprive him of the rightful fruits of his labours by promoting Wallace K. Harrison, a Rockefeller relative, rather than Corbu, to be chief architect of the UN project; and, finally, he came to believe that most American businessmen were 'gangsters' and that one had to be eternally vigilant in one's dealing with them. This just about represents his position today.

In a sense, Corbu has always carried on an unhappy love affair with America. America at first represented all the things he believed in most passionately; after his first trip he realized that America was not, perhaps, all that he had hoped, but that the *possibilities* of achieving his objective did, at least, exist in the U.S. to a degree found nowhere else. But when Corbu tried – again and again, clumsily, tactlessly, arrogantly, but, in reality, so very desperately – to work in America and to practise on a great scale what he had preached so long and so ardently, he found himself rejected wherever he turned. That this rejection was due, in large part, to the fact that in a 'teamwork age' the individual, eccentric artist is hard to assimilate, Corbu could not be expected to accept. For one thing, he considers himself to be entirely reasonable – and, of course, he is, within his terms of reference. For another, he does not really believe that committees ever produce great architecture – and in that belief he is entirely correct. Yet, to the managerial type, who is generally entrusted with great projects, any man likely to 'cause trouble' is anathema. Corbu has caused plenty in his time – and his time is better off for it.

To put it mildly, the love affair between Corbu and America did not get off to a very successful start in 1936. When he returned to France after his stay in the U.S., Corbu wrote a charming and lyrical book – *When the Cathedrals Were White* – which was, in reality, a sort of love letter to America. It was a much more adult love letter than the ones contained in *Vers une architecture* (which praised U.S. technology to the skies); but it was still an affirmation of love for all the great potentialities of the United States. Moreover, it was a touching request for the chance to prove his affection.

FIFTEEN

The late thirties were a busy and exciting time for Corbu. Everybody in Europe was, of course, aware of the likelihood of war in the near future, and many artists seemed to feel the need to complete as much of their life's work as possible before the coming of the expected holocaust. After his visit to the U.S., Corbu made a trip to Rio, where a group of architects, under the 'grand old man' of Brazilian architecture, Lucio Costa, had banded together for the design of the new building for the Ministry of Education and Health [33]. The group asked Corbu to come in as a consultant – possibly a rather reckless gesture on its part, as Corbu has a way of dominating any situation in which he finds himself. At Rio he was soon the dominant influence, designing first a long slab building rather like his Centrosoyus in Moscow, and later, after the site preferred by him turned out to be unavailable, a taller slab for a more confined lot. The Ministry sketched by Corbu was built substantially as proposed by him, and completed in 1945. By that time Costa, an extremely modest and self-effacing man, had virtually withdrawn from active participation in the group's work, as he realized that Corbu was obviously going to be the dominant spirit – whether he was physically present or not. During the development of the project a young Brazilian, Oscar Niemeyer, who had been rather a quiet and reticent participant in the planning of the building prior to Corbu's arrival, suddenly blossomed forth, under the influence of Corbu's stimulating presence, as a brilliant designer in his own right. Today the Ministry of Education building is often referred to as the work, primarily, of this remarkable young Brazilian; indeed, with its completion, Niemeyer suddenly became the outstanding young architect in South America, and he is now in charge of most of the design of Brasilia, the country's fantastic new capital. Interestingly enough, the competition for the site plan of Brasilia was won by none other than Niemeyer's original mentor, Lucio Costa; and Niemeyer, who remained intensely loyal to both Costa and Le Corbusier throughout some trying periods, is again happily working with the former on

33. *Ministry of Education and Health, Rio de Janeiro, 1936–45. The first real skyscraper designed by Le Corbusier (in association with Lucio Costa, Oscar Niemeyer, et al.). This slab building on stilts, with sun-control louvres and a sculptural roof-treatment, was the forerunner of hundreds of similar structures built since then in all parts of the world. (Photo: G. E. Kidder Smith)*

one of the largest projects to have been entrusted to any architect in the present century. Costa, incidentally, with the magnanimity of true greatness, celebrated the completion of the Ministry building by writing a letter to Corbu which acknowledged, in effect, that Corbu's work on that structure had dramatically changed the direction of Brazilian architecture.

The Ministry of Education represents an important crystallization of several of Corbu's key ideas; in general concept, it is very similar to the Swiss Pavilion – though seventeen storeys high, rather than a mere five. Like the Swiss Pavilion, it is a slab building on *pilotis*, with a rather free-shaped assembly and exhibition-hall structure 'slid' under the tall, elevated, rectangular prism at ground floor. Like the Swiss Pavilion, the Ministry of Education also has short, blank end walls and long, glassy side walls; but, *unlike* the Swiss Pavilion, the Ministry has a handsome grille of movable *brises-soleil* covering the entire height and width of its sunny (north) façade. Finally, like the Swiss Pavilion and like the Villa Savoye, the Ministry building has a magnificently plastic superstructure of penthouses containing mechanical equipment, restaurants, and recreation areas – all set in a handsome roof garden.

Although Corbu had been working with the concept of sun-control louvres for several years prior to 1936, the Ministry of Education in Rio was the first large building to make full use of this device. Since that time the combination of a glass 'curtain wall' protected by a grille of sun-control devices – vertical, horizontal, circular, or what have you – has become a standard solution for modern buildings. Properly designed, this outside curtain of sun louvres can keep the interior cool without seriously obstructing the view of the outdoors. Even in fully air-conditioned buildings such sun-control devices have helped drastically to reduce the air-conditioning load and cost. Throughout the tropical and semi-tropical areas of the world Corbu's *brises-soleil* are now an accepted and proven architectural device.

The Ministry of Education was probably the largest building constructed according to Corbu's design in the years immediately preceding the Second World War. At the same time, he was so busy on so many other projects and structures during those years that it is impossible to mention them all. There were more projects for North Africa, including some designs for a three-winged skyscraper, generally Y-shaped in plan, which suggested a more varied urban silhouette than that offered by slab buildings; and there were several exhibitions, including a steel-and-canvas structure – Le Pavillon des Temps Nouveaux – put up for the Paris World's Fair of 1937.

This light and colourful bit of playfulness was one of the first modern buildings to be based upon the recognition that steel is strongest in tension. The roof – a translucent canvas sheet that permitted diffused light to enter the pavilion – was supported entirely on cables suspended between the uprights and left to assume their natural, catenary curve. The technical principle Corbu demonstrated here in an almost off-hand way is now being applied to tension structures all over the world – by men like the young American architect Paul Rudolph, who has built several such structures in Florida, and by others who feel that the tensile strength of steel strands, demonstrated again and again in our own suspension bridges, has enormous potentialities. In other designs for exhibition pavilions prepared during that period, Corbu and Jeanneret developed systems of so-called space frames of light steel, used both in tension and in compression, which were engineered much like aeroplane wings. Here again Corbu suggested a new structural form, which has not been further developed, both in concrete and steel, by younger architects in the U.S. and elsewhere. Unfortunately, Corbu was again too early; in 1939 nobody in authority was willing to commission this sort of exhibition structure, despite the fact that exhibitions, from the Crystal Palace Exhibition onwards, had been traditional proving grounds for experimental architecture.

Throughout the years immediately before the Second World War, when virtually nothing was being built in a world hypnotized by the gradual build-up of Hitler's attack, Corbu was bursting with ideas, each more challenging than the one preceding it. For Philippeville, in French North Africa, he designed a museum whose plan was like a square snail or square spiral, flattened out and, by its nature, infinite in terms of possible future expansion. This idea has been picked up in different ways by others; even Frank Lloyd Wright's postwar Guggenheim Museum probably owes a good deal to this project or to its predecessor, Corbu's *ascending* spiral museum of 1929. Corbu, the painter, knew more than any other architect of his time about ways and means of lighting a painting; and the Philippeville snail was illuminated entirely by skylights that followed the plan pattern all around the roof. Corbu had to wait for almost twenty years to get a chance to build this museum; finally, in 1958, the structure first designed in 1939 was built by him in Ahmedabad, in India, and another was completed in Tokyo in the same year.

34. *Monument for Vaillant-Couturier, 1938. This composition of geometric and naturalistic forms shows Le Corbusier taking a dramatically new direction in his work.* (*Courtesy, Museum of Modern Art*)

Then there was the sketch for a monument, in 1937, to be erected in the memory of Vaillant-Couturier [34], the veteran French Communist deputy and first editor of *L'Humanité*. Vaillant-Couturier was the sort of idealistic Communist who vanished from the scene after the Hitler–Stalin pact. A competition was held for the design of a monument to him, to be built at the intersection of two great highways leading into Paris, and Corbu was one of those who submitted an entry to the competition jury. His submission was highly sculptural, an entirely plastic, poetic object of monumental proportions. The composition was quite abstract, with only two representational elements in it: a giant hand, palm open to the sky in the manner that seemed to spell 'man against the world'; and a head, also gigantic, that showed the veteran Communist crying out against injustice. These two naturalistic elements were placed, quite abstractly, into a composition of slabs and frames of concrete – a composition of violently beautiful contrasts, of brilliant, searing-white sunlight, and sombre, near-black shade. Like all of Corbu's earlier competition entries, this one was rejected by the jury; yet, in 1945, when the Museum of Modern Art in New York began to face up to the fact

107

that a new rash of war memorials was about to be visited upon the U.S., it decided to exhibit Corbu's great monumental project as an example of what might be done.

The monument to Vaillant-Couturier was particularly significant in this respect; Corbu, who had started as a painter of cubes and spheres and prisms, was now quite evidently determined to bring certain elements of nature – even representational art – back into sculpture, architecture, and, indeed, painting. While the basic composition of the monument was still quite Cubist in feeling, no Cubist who valued his membership in the 'club' would have seriously considered including a representation of a human head and a human hand in a composition of this sort. In Corbu's development as a complete artist, this move towards naturalism had been under way for some ten years or so. 'Beginning in 1928,' he said later, 'I threw open a window on the human figure.' Some years earlier he had added pebbles, pieces of wood, meat bones, and roots of trees – 'objects evoking poetic reactions' – to the precise, Cubist forms found earlier in his paintings. Now the human figure was back in his paintings – and in his sculpture as well. Indeed, Corbu could hardly be called an uncompromising Machine Art man any longer; in all his work, from the late twenties on, there were unmistakable signs of a loosening-up process, a growing interest in nature as a source of inspiration. In 1937, for example, when Corbu consented again to show his paintings and sculpture (after an absence from the galleries of a dozen years), the visitors to the Kunsthaus in Zürich were amazed to see a fluidity of line and form, and a preoccupation with the *human* form, which seemed to have little in common with the Purist paintings done by Corbu in the early twenties.

This growing fluidity of line and form, coupled with an increasing use of natural materials, should have been apparent to Corbu's admirers for some time: the 1930 plan for Algiers, with its huge, curvilinear apartment and office buildings; the intense plasticity of forms in Corbu's own apartment, built between 1930 and 1933; the free-form patterns that increasingly dominated Corbu's landscape plans for his great urban projects of the 1930s – all these were ample indications that the rigidity of cube, cone, and sphere was being superseded by a much less self-conscious and more varied vocabulary of forms. Indeed, only the outbreak of the Second World War kept Corbu from entering upon an entirely new phase in his architectural development.

SIXTEEN

As he did during the First World War, Corbu used the years of enforced idleness primarily to paint and to develop new ideas on paper. In a small vacation house at Cap Martin in the Alpes Maritimes, Corbu was at work on a number of murals when the Second World War came. For several months, to everybody's surprise, the existence of a state of war made relatively little difference to daily life in France. Naturally, nothing was being built, though much was being projected. Yet life continued in a rather placid manner. Corbu was used to painting under almost any conditions and in many kinds of places – on trains, on ships, in hotel rooms – and he had developed a typically orderly method of allocating time to his painting. 'For seven years I was able to give only Saturday afternoons and Sundays to painting,' he once explained. 'Then, later, until the war, I was able to paint every morning from eight to one.' An artist – i.e., presumably a rebel – who paints according to a rigid timetable is, surely, one of the more amusing inventions of the watchmaking Swiss! In any event, Corbu continued to paint during the first months of the war, both in the south of France and in Paris, giving more time to this aspect of his work than he had been able to do before.

Then, suddenly, in May 1940 the Germans attacked. Corbu left Paris and went south to the Pyrenees. With the defeat of France, it became more and more difficult to obtain pigments, and his painting began to slow down. Like many others, he hoped that preparatory work for the postwar reconstruction of France could be done in the months and years ahead; but the authorities at Vichy proved to be impossible to work with. Yet, because they were the only authorities potentially interested in postwar reconstruction, Corbu had to deal with them for a while. During this period, particularly while Corbu prepared another of his brilliant and hopeful projects for the re-development of Algiers, people outside France heard rumours to the effect that he had become a collaborationist. One architectural magazine in New York actually printed the report, although Corbu's 'political history' should have warned everyone that he was highly unlikely to conform to any existing political coloration. In 1928, when he designed the Centrosoyus for Moscow, he had been denounced as a Communist; by 1931, when his project for a Palace of the Soviets was rejected in favour of a neo-classical wedding cake of fantastic proportions, Corbu denounced the Soviets as uncivilized; then, in 1942, when he was about to present his latest plan for Algiers to the Municipal Council of that city, the Vichy authorities decided that he was a Communist and rejected his proposal – at the very moment when so-called liberal architects in the U.S. and Britain decided that Corbu was, in fact, a Fascist collaborator. And, when the war was over, Corbu often talked vaguely to visiting Americans about his belief that some sort of 'communist' brotherhood of man was the only answer – so there he was a Communist again! But as the Soviet line on architecture had become violently anti-Corbu, the Soviet *New Times*, meanwhile, was denouncing him as a bourgeois reactionary; indeed, the Soviet architect Shkvarikov, who visited Switzerland in 1948, announced that Corbu's apartments at Geneva 'looked like an absurd, alien growth', had 'nothing in common with the people', and were therefore 'doomed to wither away'! Finally, in the early fifties, Corbu became a Fascist again in the pages of certain American women's magazines (because his architecture was so 'inhuman'); he became a Communist again in the pages of *Time*; and he will, undoubtedly, become a good many other things depending upon the prevailing 'liberal' or 'reactionary' attitudes of magazine editors towards such real or potential clients of Le Corbusier as Nehru, De Gaulle, the Emperor of Japan, or the current dictator of Iraq.

The facts are that Corbu is totally disinterested in politics; that he finds it necessary, at times, to deal with politicians in order to achieve certain important objectives of planning and redevelopment; and that his own 'political' philosophy has to do with such issues as the continuity of civilization on earth and the need for assuring such continuity – concerns that are not easily labelled in terms of today's political pressure-groups.

Among the many projects of the war years, there was one in particular which represented a powerful new direction in his work. As part of one of his Algiers projects, Corbu designed a skyscraper of fifty-odd storeys to serve as a central administration building for the port [35]. This tower was lozenge-shaped in plan, very much like the Rentenanstalt project developed by Corbu in 1933 for Zürich. As in that earlier insurance-company building, the reason for the plan shape was simply that the centre of the building was taken up by space-consuming stacks of lifts and other services, so that it seemed reasonable to fatten up the building around its core to accommodate an adequate amount of office space around the entire periphery of the plan.

Apart from the similarity in plan, however, the Algiers tower had very little in common with the Rentenanstalt. The latter was to have been a very slick and glassy building – a volume enclosed by a smooth curtain wall of glass. But the Algiers building was anything but smooth; instead of the slick, glassy skin designed for the Zürich building, this monumental tower was to have a deep egg-crate pattern of concrete *brises-soleil* all over its façades. But, even more importantly, the façades were anything but regular, for the egg-crate pattern was full of variations in scale, and it was punctured, more or less at will, with dramatic spaces hollowed out of the mass of the tower, forming great terraces and gardens dozens of storeys up in the sky. Corbu's model for this tower suggested something else which he was to develop in actual buildings after the war: for it seems that the Algiers skyscraper was meant to be built of rough, unfinished concrete, rather than smoothly finished with stucco or stone veneer, as were so many of Corbu's structures in the twenties and thirties.

Because the core of the Algiers tower was a vertical shaft of lifts, and the most important structural element was the load-bearing row of columns surrounding that core, Corbu compared the building to a tree – i.e., a structure with a central trunk, with branches extending out from that trunk (the office floors), and with roots firmly anchored in the ground (the foundations). Obvious as this analogy may seem, it was anything but obvious to have been brought up by someone who had originally reacted against the naturalistic preferences of Art Nouveau. Frank Lloyd Wright, of course, had always used the tree analogy to describe his tall buildings, and he was to use it most effectively in describing two of his postwar projects of the 1950s – the Price tower in Bartlesville, Oklahoma, and the fantastic Mile High building projected for Chicago's Lake Shore. But, then, Wright had never strayed far from Art Nouveau anyway, whereas Corbu had opposed the movement almost as vigorously as he had opposed neo-classicism.

But, as in his paintings and sculpture, the lessons that could be learned from nature were beginning to become increasingly important to his architectural work. His buildings still looked entirely man-made – and they always would. But the principles of continuous structure and of interrelated proportion which Corbu began to see everywhere in nature took over from his earlier infatuation with the machine.

35. Projected skyscraper for Algiers, 1938–42. This concrete-grille tower, lozenge-shaped in plan, is Le Corbusier's first major departure from 'graph-paper' façades. The interrupted pattern of the concrete grille is determined by a system of identical proportions – *rather than identical* dimensions. (*From* Œuvre complète)

With the liberation of Paris, Corbu returned to the capital to try and start again. He found the roof garden outside his apartment overgrown with weeds – an aspect that seemed quite poetic to him. 'My garden has been allowed to run wild,' he wrote, 'the rosebushes have become large eglantines; the wind, the bees have brought seeds; a laburnum has grown; a sycamore; lavender bushes have spread out. The turf has become coarse grass. The wind and sun control the composition, half man, half nature . . .' There was little coal in Paris, and Corbu would stand in his icy studio, wrapped in a heavily lined, three-quarter-length U.S. army Mackinaw, working away on more paintings. Young American and British architects, serving in the Allied armies, would pass through Paris and stop off to pay their respects. Mme Le Corbusier, a wonderfully simple French 'peasant' with none of Corbu's sophistication, but all the warmth and humour Corbu sometimes lacked, would occasionally cook for a visiting American soldier and make raucous and irreverent jokes while Corbu was demonstrating, very seriously, some gadget he had designed and put into his apartment years earlier. From all over the world young people inquired as to Corbu's whereabouts: how he had managed to live through the war (he had been seriously sick for a while, but was now back in fairly good shape); how his buildings had survived the bombings and shellings (some very well, others badly); what his plans were for the future.

To Corbu himself, the end of the war was, quite simply, a signal to get going, full blast, with the reconstruction of Europe. There was not a moment to lose. 'There are ruins, stones overthrown, frustrated ideas. The universal forge is working at full speed. Give it jobs to do! Work! Let us create the tools of happiness – the equipment for a modern world!' He had a tremendous sense of urgency, yet he also sensed that many opportunities were about to be missed. 'France, are you going to withdraw your head and your horns into your shell, like a snail?' he asked. The answer was perhaps not quite as simple as Corbu thought, for there were immediate problems of housing those without any sort of shelter, of restoring buildings that still could be saved, of simply providing the minimal necessities.

Whatever the problems and delays, Corbu decided that he could not wait, that too much had to be done. The war was hardly over when he began to work on two major projects: the new city plan for Saint-Dié, in the Vosges Mountains of France; and a large apartment project to be built for bombed-out families in the suburbs of Marseille. These two projects – the first never built, the second completed in 1952 – were the culmination of Le Corbusier's work over more than three decades; and they eclipse in importance most of the city planning and housing work done in Europe prior to that time.

To understand what this means, it must be remembered that Corbu was now almost sixty years old; that he was no longer in the best of health; that much of his work of the twenties and thirties had remained unbuilt, and thus might have simply served as a reservoir, a backlog of existing and well-studied ideas that one could draw upon now at will and rework slightly to fit an immediate situation. In short, Corbu had done his bit – and much more – for modern architecture, and might well be permitted to rest on his laurels.

He did nothing of the sort: at Saint-Dié and at Marseille he created two concepts of such staggering boldness and beauty that most of his devoted followers in other parts of the world were left far behind, still playing around with the forms of a Ville Contemporaine or a Swiss Pavilion of the twenties and thirties. Corbu, far from settling down to the peaceful role of an elder statesman, had opened up several new vistas. Fifteen years later the younger architects of Europe, Asia, and the Americas were only just beginning to grasp the lessons of Saint-Dié and Marseille.

During the war the historic centre of Saint-Dié had been destroyed systematically by the Germans. They had evacuated some 10,000 inhabitants and then, over a period of three days and three nights, had razed the core of the town, block by block, with hand grenades and mines. After the liberation, officials of the town asked Corbu to work on the reconstruction of its old centre.

Corbu's unrealized proposal [36] covered an area approximately one mile square. To the south the area was defined by the river Meurthe, and on all sides around the periphery of the centre, there were highways linking Saint-Dié to Nancy, Strasbourg, and other

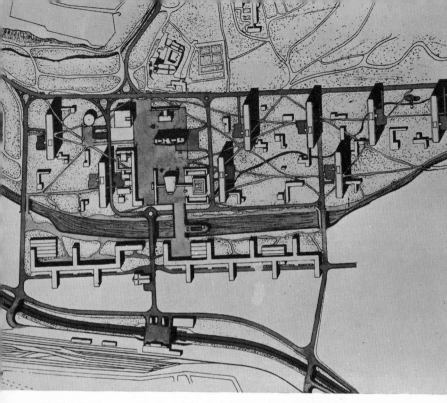

36. Plan for the reconstruction of the centre of Saint-Dié, 1945. The proposal for the monumental plaza has influenced every important city plan since 1945. (Courtesy, Museum of Modern Art)

major cities. Corbu proposed to locate manufacturing plants to the south of the river, and large apartment blocks to the east of the central area. All this was well and reasonably worked out; but it was the civic centre itself, along the north bank of the Meurthe, that showed Corbu at his finest.

This centre was to have been a magnificent pedestrian plaza, reached from all directions by ramps and bridges, surrounded by parking facilities, and facing the river to the south. The plaza was monumental in scale: its east and west limits were defined by tall apartment slabs, about 1,000 feet apart. Between these tall slabs, which framed the plaza, Corbu proposed to place a series of buildings of varying shape and form, each, in a sense, a huge piece of sculpture set into this paved and landscaped sculpture garden. To the north, impressively tall and robust like some giant campanile, there was to have been an office tower to contain the administrative functions of city government. This tower was differentiated from the apartment slabs by its lozenge-shaped plan, similar to that of the tower Corbu had designed for Algiers three years earlier. Like the Algiers tower, this one had an irregular egg-crate façade, penetrated here and there by great terraces and other volumes and forms meant to symbolize certain ceremonial functions of civic government. The great administrative tower was on an axis with one of the automobile approaches to the civic centre, and visible from every part of town. It was, in a sense, the 'cathedral' of a modern town – the central symbol that makes the core of a city also its heart.

Between the great tower and the banks of the river, there were to have been several lower structures: restaurants, stores, a wedge-shaped civic auditorium, and a square museum with Corbu's characteristic snail plan. Beyond these lower structures the plaza extended farther to the south in a broad, pedestrian bridge that spanned the Meurthe and led to a large swimming-pool 'carved' out of the river. The composition of these different structures, and the composition of landscaping and paving patterns, was entirely asymmetrical. Yet, despite its inherently dynamic qualities, the composition was in monumental repose – a classic outdoor space as serene as any of the great Renaissance piazzas.

Although the plaza for Saint-Dié was formed as carefully as a sculpture collection, it should not be thought for a moment that it was abstractly conceived, without regard for human scale. Characteristically, Corbu measured his drawings for Saint-Dié not only with the standard metric scale, but, more importantly, with a scale indicating the distance a man might be able to traverse on foot in a quarter of an hour. Moreover, to anyone willing to imagine himself in the position of walking through this great civic centre, another extraordinary dimension becomes immediately apparent: this is the dimension of surprise, of changing vistas, of sudden turns around a corner leading towards an entirely unexpected and quite stunning new perspective. This is a centre designed entirely in four dimensions, planned to be walked through, to be a delight to the eye of man, whose line of vision might be about sixty-three inches above the ground – not to the eye of a bird or a model-maker, whose perspective has distorted so much urban design in recent decades.

The Saint-Dié plan has served as *the* model for almost every great modern civic centre projected since 1945. The elements proposed by Corbu have often been copied too slavishly, too insensitively and two-dimensionally. Yet in many parts of the world where plans for new 'hearts' of cities are drawn, Corbu's vision of a great new piazza for Saint-Dié has dominated all thinking over the past fifteen years.

This is so not only because of the inherent merits of the Saint-Dié proposal; it is so, to a large extent, because Corbu's project for Saint-Dié was a reaffirmation, at exactly the right moment, of his belief – and the belief of many of his contemporaries – that the great city, the metropolis, could be a supremely beautiful thing. Let the Garden City dreamers build their endless rows of detached cottages; let the agrarians rant against the evils of high urban densities. The facts of life, Corbu seemed to feel, would catch up with them soon enough. Meanwhile, let us make a demonstration of how magnificent a modern city can be, how great a heart we can give it, how *human* we can make its scale. Saint-Dié said all this and more; it was the most persuasive argument for urban greatness a modern architect has ever been able to put on paper.

While this city plan was discussed and exhibited in many parts of the world, local politics in the town of Saint-Dié once again intervened – and Corbu's proposal was rejected. He did build a small industrial structure in the town, but no part of his great plan was ever accepted and realized. As so often in the past, Corbu found himself snubbed, his finest ideas rejected by politicians of every stripe. In place of his proposal, a trite, neo-classical plan was finally accepted. Dr Sigfried Giedion closes this particular chapter in Corbu's life with the flat statement that Corbu's plan for Saint-Dié, 'for the first time in our period, would have presented a crystallization of community life . . . [equal to] the Greek meeting place . . .'

The Marseille apartment building, however, did get built [37] though it took much time and much energy to overcome man-made obstacles. Corbu's great mentor on this project was the French Minister for Reconstruction, Eugène Claudius-Petit, who fought many a battle for the Marseille building when every other authority seemed to turn against it.

In a schematic sense, the Marseille building is a summation of everything Corbu had advocated in connexion with urban living from 1920 onwards. It is a huge slab, 450 feet long, sixty-six feet thick, and about 200 feet tall. It contains almost 340 apartments for some 1,600 people. It has fifteen apartment floors in all, plus a two-storey 'shop-

37. *Apartment block at Marseille, 1946–52. This gigantic, concrete city on sculptured stilts has two shopping streets halfway up, and elaborate communal facilities on the roof. Each apartment has a two-storey-high balcony at one end. Dividing walls between balconies were painted in bright pastel shades.* (*Photo: G. E. Kidder Smith*)

ping street' that runs down the length of the building, about one third of the way up. Two rows of Corbu's inevitable *pilotis* hold up the monumental slab; there are the equally inevitable two-storey living-rooms in each apartment, backed up with two storeys of bedrooms and service areas; and above it all is the communal roof garden – the piazza up in the sky – where the inhabitants of this single, vertical city may meet and talk and watch their children play.

All of this is, of course, simply a crystallization of Corbu's basic beliefs throughout the twenties and thirties. The sole extraordinary fact about the *planning* of the Marseille building is the proof it again affords of Corbu's almost fanatical single-mindedness over the years – his extraordinarily sharp and precise vision, from the days when he began to sketch out his ideas to the moment when his admirers

38. Detail of fire-escape on Marseille apartments. The concrete shows the rough imprint of wooden forms. (Photo: Lucien Hervé)

watched the Marseille building go up and hailed it as the ultimate revelation of architectural truth. For this building is an absolutely logical extension of Corbu's 'superimposed villas' and of his Pavilion de l'Esprit Nouveau – both designed more than twenty years earlier. And every detail in the planning of the Marseille building had, indeed, been clarified by Corbu many years before.

Why, then, is the Marseille building so much more than a mere summary of Corbu's development over the years? Why is it so startling a departure both for him and for modern architecture as a whole?

To understand the reasons for this, it is necessary for a moment to recall what architects in the West were doing and thinking during the Second World War. Among the best indices to their thinking are two issues of the American magazine *Architectural Forum*, which invited several dozen U.S. architects in 1943 to project on paper their ideas for a postwar architecture. Their proposals were published under the heading of 'Building for 194x', and they covered every conceivable type of structure, from a 'disposable house' to a library stocking nothing but microfilm editions and equipped with electronic brains. What all these rather delightful dreams had in common was this: they all assumed that the postwar world would be one of fabulously finished, beautifully manufactured and engineered synthetics – building components of aluminium, plastics, and glass. Everything was going to be slicker, smoother, more industrialized, more rational – in short, more Machine Art than ever before.

Well, 194x had come at last, and Le Corbusier, the leading apostle of Machine Art, was surely going to show the world what the machine could *really* achieve in terms of industrial precision.

Instead, Corbu did the exact opposite: he built his first entirely timeless building. The Marseille structure is all concrete – concrete in its crudest, most brutal form, *le béton brut*. Concrete poured into the simplest form work, to come out looking as rough and virile as rock, deliberately chipped and cracked, full of pebble surfaces here and sea-shell surfaces there, as beautifully textured as the now blackened travertine of the great Roman ruins of Italy and southern France. Next to the Marseille building, Lever House would look like the latest Cadillac – slick, thin-shelled, soon out of date. Next to the Marseille building, every other modern 'curtain wall' structure would

look as tinny as an oil can, and sure to rust away just as fast. For this massive piece of brute concrete could be of any time: it could be an Egyptian temple of 2000 B.C., or a vision of the twenty-first century.

Why had Corbu shifted to so earthy, so 'organic' a way of building? There were, undoubtedly, a number of practical reasons: he had discovered after the war that many of his earlier buildings, whose finishes had turned out to be something less than permanent, looked depressingly tired after their stucco façades had become streaky and grey. With his intuitive sense of tradition and of historical continuity, Corbu had begun to feel the need for building materials that would age well. Next, there was another purely practical reason – the lower cost of unfinished concrete. And, finally, there was the equally simple and practical fact that the modern materials promised for the postwar world were just not available in France.

Still, all these reasons could have been overcome. Other European architects, faced with similar realizations in the postwar years, simply turned back to traditional materials and details for their building vocabulary. But Corbu, of course, was wedded to concrete. Not only because it was a 'modern' material, but because it was the most plastic and expressively sculptural material at hand – and, moreover, the only material that, in the French building economy, could offer the essential city-planning device of the *pilotis* and the essential interior planning device of the free and flexible plan. He felt that the potentialities of reinforced concrete had barely been explored: the material was clearly capable of such great variety in texture and colour that there was no need whatever to finish it by applying coats of stucco or paint. And he had found out that the wooden forms into which the concrete must be poured need not be constructed of smoothly finished sheets of plywood, but could be built of rough boards, nailed together with slightly open joints, to leave an imprint of lines and even of wood grain upon the hardened surface of the material.

To many American visitors, in particular, who were used to slick finishes in their buildings, the Marseille structure seemed to be crude and sloppy. But this is not the case at all; in a sense, this structure is a deliberate affirmation of man in a Machine Art era. The man-made imprint on concrete, according to Corbu, seemed to 'shout at one from all parts of the structure'. Indeed, he stated at the great ceremonial opening of the building that 'it seems to be really possible to consider concrete as a reconstructed stone worthy of being exposed in its natural state'.

The gigantic slab rising up behind a row of trees along the boulevard Michelet outside Marseille looks as graceful as Joe Louis on tiptoe. It is supported on rows of sculptured and tapered *pilotis*, two storeys high and as grandiose as the columns of Karnak. The slab itself (unlike most American slab buildings of the postwar years) is faced with an *irregular* egg crate, the irregularity being the result, in part, of the fact that the rows of two-storey living-rooms face alternately east and west (the two-storey apartments interlock back and forth in the cross-section of the building). While the rough concrete of the structure has a natural, pinkish-grey tint, the wall panels that separate adjoining balconies were painted in bright pastel colours – red, blue, yellow, and near-black. These are part of Corbu's beautiful palette – 'what I call the "great gamut", the earth colours and ochres, ultramarine, white and black', he once said. And he added: 'We used to say, "If you wish to paint black, take your tube of white; if you wish to paint white, take your tube of black."' These plastic colours, not applied flat to the façade, but seen only through a sort of veil that represents the imaginary façade of the building, give the slab an added sense of three-dimensionality.

But it was really the roof garden [39], more than any other part of this building, that set the Marseille structure apart from anything that Corbu, or anyone else, had done before. This roof garden is a huge plaza, bordered by a high parapet, and filled with intensely sculptural elements – great tapered funnels through which the air is exhausted from the building; vaulted structures that house a gymnasium; a concrete mountain range full of tunnels and caves, designed for children to play in; a nursery school, a pool, a restaurant, a row of curved concrete benches for mothers to sit on while watching their babies; a bold, free-standing vertical concrete slab on which to project films at night; and a cantilevered balcony (the only element that punctures the high parapet) designed for lovers who might like to sit there in privacy and watch the sunset. This sculpture garden has been compared to all sorts of things: to the fantasies of the French eighteenth-century architect Claude-Nicholas Ledoux, whose marvellous geometric forms seem today a preview of the Machine Art era; and to the equally fantastic creations of the nineteenth-century architect Antonio Gaudí, whose Parc Güell may, quite possibly, have influenced Corbu when he saw it during one of his frequent visits to Barcelona.

But the greatness of the roof garden on the Marseille building has little to do with traceable influences. The whole thing is an original, creative work of sculpture. The Marseille building is situated in a rather unattractive suburb; yet the roof garden, being surrounded by a high parapet, appears to be a strangely dreamlike piazza, located in space, suspended somewhere between the silhouettes of the Alpes Maritimes and the distant view of the Mediterranean and the Château d'If. It is, in a way, a modern sort of Acropolis. Corbu, when first visiting the Acropolis during one of his early trips through south-east Europe, had been overwhelmed by the grandeur of that sculptural abstraction raised up against the sky. He recalls saying to himself: 'Remember the clear, clean, intense, economical, violent Parthenon – that cry hurled into a landscape made of grace and terror. That monument to strength and purity.' And at Marseille, some forty years later, he succeeded in matching that 'monument to strength and purity' in his own way.

Corbu is a mixture of many things. He is an artist of incredible strength; a fighter of great passions; a pamphleteer of tremendous eloquence. He needed all these qualities to accomplish Marseille: he must have written half a dozen books and pamphlets about this building, fought many more battles for it (at one time during the construction of the Marseille project some delightfully archaic Society for the Preservation of the Beauties of France tried to have him forcibly restrained from despoiling his nation). Yet, to him, one of the happiest achievements at Marseille was a 1,000-foot-long cinder track that he was able to incorporate in the design of his roof garden. Corbu is a very wiry and *sportif* type, and he enjoyed this track almost as much as he enjoyed everything else about the building, posing proudly for photographers while trotting around his great 'piazza on the roof', attired only in shorts, a sweatshirt, and a very professional-looking pair of track shoes. Obviously Corbu has always been very serious about becoming a 'complete man'.

There was a great celebration on the Marseille roof when the building 'officially' opened, at a CIAM party on a summer evening in 1953. Architects from every part of the world attended, including Corbu's old associate from the days in Behrens's office, Walter Gropius, who had by this time become the principal apostle of Machine Art architecture in the United States. Yet Gropius recognized at once that Corbu had created an entirely new architectural vocabulary. 'Any architect who does not find this building beautiful,' Gropius said on that evening, 'had better lay down his pencil.'

39. Part of roof garden above Marseille apartments. The foothills of the Alps are just visible above the high roof parapets. (Photo: Richard Miller)

EIGHTEEN

Corbu became best known to people in the U.S. in the years after the end of the Second World War, when he served as the representative of France on the United Nations Headquarters Commission. (He had become a French citizen in 1930.) The job of this Commission was to select the site for the proposed UN Headquarters; and by the end of 1946 it agreed to accept an offer by John D. Rockefeller, Jr, of a seventeen-acre site located along the East River in Manhattan. Corbu published a little book on the job of selecting the site (as he was apt to do on just about every other job that came along), and that made it official, at least in his mind.

Following his work on the Commission, Le Corbusier became one of the ten architects selected from all over the world who were to plan the actual Headquarters buildings. Throughout the spring and the summer of 1947 Corbu was in New York, working feverishly to realize one of his greatest and oldest ambitions – to build a seat for a potential world government. It seemed to him that he was about to be compensated for the severe and unjust blow he had received at the time of the League of Nations competition; and it further seemed to him that the job of designing the UN Headquarters should very properly be his. For, after all, the very fact that here the authorities had turned to a group of *modern* rather than traditional architects represented final proof that the new architecture had won its battles. And no one had done more than Corbu to help win those battles – or so he felt.

To Corbu, the moral issue was quite clear: the UN had to be his; he deserved every bit of it! To partisans of Frank Lloyd Wright, of course, the moral issue was equally clear: Wright, rather than Corbu, had won the battle for modern architecture, so he was the obvious choice for the design of the UN Headquarters.

As things worked out, neither Corbu nor Wright was awarded the job. Once a site in the heart of Manhattan had been chosen, Wright was never seriously considered. His hostility towards the city was only too well known; and he had made no secret of his views of the proposed East River site. 'Grass the ground where the proposed UN sky-scraper would stand,' Wright announced, characteristically. 'Buy a befitting tract of land, say a thousand acres or more, not too easy to reach . . . Sequester the UN. Why does it not itself ask for good ground where nature speaks and the beauty of organic order shows more clearly the true pattern of all peace whatsoever?' But the UN authorities were not willing to grass the ground and move out into the prairie; they *wanted* to be in New York, they *liked* the metropolis, they had no intention of sequestering themselves.

The basic decision about the character of the UN Headquarters was made almost without debate: the Headquarters was going to be urban, which meant that it would have to be designed by architects basically in sympathy with the city. So long as everyone was agreed that the architecture should be modern, this meant, almost inevitably, that it should be of the International Style.

Next, there were the obvious political problems: should the UN job go to a single architect? If there had been some degree of decisiveness and courage in places of authority, the answer might conceivably have been in the affirmative – in which case Corbu would, in all likelihood, have been chosen by general acclamation (including his own). But those in high places at the UN felt that an international Board of Design should be selected, to consist of ten architects from ten major countries: Corbu was chosen to represent France, Oscar Niemeyer to represent Brazil, Sven Markelius to represent his native Sweden, and several less well-known architects represented the U.S.S.R., Belgium, Canada, China, Great Britain, Australia, and Uruguay. The next logical step was to select a chairman; and here again a politically sound choice was made in the selection of the American architect Wallace K. Harrison. There were several reasons for the choice of Harrison: first, everyone realized that the Headquarters would certainly involve some very large structures, and Harrison's experience in the design of Rockefeller Center was bound to be very useful. Second, it was felt that an American should be the chairman, as no one outside the U.S. had had very much experience with the purely technical problems involved in constructing very tall buildings. And, third, it was recognized that the chairmanship of such a Board of Design would call for a man with the wisdom of Solomon; and while Harrison may not have measured up to that standard in every respect, no one in authority could think of another American architect who came closer to filling those specifications than he.

The result of all this careful diplomacy was exactly what might have been expected. From the very beginning Corbu's dynamic, indeed crackling personality dominated the situation. There were virtually no projects developed by any of the participants which did not, basically, reflect Corbu's concepts. The only disagreements in principle seem to have concerned matters of relative detail. All members of the Board of Design agreed that: (a) the Secretariat would have to be a tall, slablike building; (b) the General Assembly structure would be a relatively low and free form, derived largely from the pie-shaped assembly halls contained within it; and (c) the Meeting Halls would be contained within another low structure that somehow joined the Secretariat to the General Assembly. All were agreed, also, that there would be some sort of plaza and that the Delegations building then planned (but not immediately built) would be another slab (or, possibly, two slabs) that would help form that plaza in conjunction with the Secretariat.

This general layout is an almost exact duplicate of Le Corbusier's first 1936 project for the Rio Ministry of Education. No one could possibly deny this, and no one did. Yet Corbu wanted to be recognized as the sole designer of the UN Headquarters, not only in theory, but also in practice. The situation became increasingly tense as Corbu tried to run the show, and for a while it was partly Niemeyer's quiet tact that kept things on a more or less even keel.

When Corbu had appeared in Rio some ten years earlier, Lucio Costa decided that it was the better part of valour to withdraw discreetly from the Ministry of Education design team. Perhaps it would have been the better part of valour for Harrison to leave the field of operations to Corbu; yet this was hardly possible, for everyone at the UN seemed to be agreed that an architect with American building know-how was required to see the job through. So Harrison stayed on; and after the Board of Design had arrived at its basic scheme, Harrison, as Director of Planning, was appointed to set up his own UN Headquarters Planning Office and to carry out the scheme developed by the Board of Design.

At this point the tension that had been building up around Corbu finally erupted into open hostility and verbal violence. Corbu announced to all the world that the design approved by the Board was actually his own proposal, which he had submitted to the Board on 15 March 1947. Corbu's proposal, identified by the number '23 A', was indeed almost identical with the project finally adopted, although that proposal also owed something to a series of sketches prepared by Niemeyer. Corbu has claimed that Scheme '23 A' formed the basis for all discussions by the Board of Design over a period of three months after he first submitted it, and this claim seems to be generally accurate. Corbu kept a sketchbook throughout the deliberations of the Board of Design, and his daily entries support the argument that it was his contribution, primarily, that shaped the UN.

As a matter of fact, there is no one who would care to argue this point, least of all, one imagines, Wallace Harrison. The point at issue in selecting the architect to *execute* the design was not whether he had made the principal contribution to its conception but, rather, whether he had shown the organizational and diplomatic ability to carry out this complex and politically difficult assignment. Regardless of how much respect one may have for Corbu's creativity, it is hard to believe that Corbu would have been a more competent over-all administrator of the job than Harrison. The fact is that few people in the past had been able to work with Corbu on any terms other than submissive adulation (which may, indeed, have been his due); and, rightly or wrongly, the UN authorities felt that they had a better chance of getting the job done competently, smoothly, and well with someone like Harrison in charge than with an 'eccentric' like Corbu running the show.

Corbu's own actions after the decision had been made hardly served to impress his critics or his admirers with his tact. He denounced Harrison, more or less publicly, as a 'gangster' who had stolen Corbu's design and made it his own. Corbu hinted darkly that Harrison's relationship by marriage to the Rockefeller family had got him the job; and he hinted, even more darkly, that the famous sketchbook he had kept during the deliberations of the Board of Design had mysteriously disappeared in 1948, when the construction drawings for the UN were being prepared under Harrison's supervision, only to reappear just as mysteriously in 1950. In short, he showed himself to be that most regrettable of social beings, a bad loser.

Corbu's attacks on Harrison were both intemperate and unfair. Harrison is one of the most modest, gentle, and scrupulously honest professionals to be found in the U.S. or anywhere else. Although many critics disagree with Harrison's design preferences, few would be willing to deny that his ability as an organizer made him a natural choice for the top position on the UN project – Rockefeller or no Rockefeller. And, finally, the idea that 'someone' might have stolen

Corbu's sketchbooks in order to copy his ideas in developing the UN drawings is patently ludicrous. All of Corbu's suggestions were plainly on record at the UN, and there was no need for cloak-and-dagger methods to unveil his innermost thoughts: Corbu has never left such thoughts unpublicized.

Yet, after all has been said about Corbu's unfortunate actions in connexion with the award to Harrison of the execution of the UN buildings, there still remains the unhappy fact that a UN Headquarters carried out by Corbu would have been a finer work of art than that standing on the East River today. For in almost every detail the UN buildings are too slick and, at the same time, too heavy-handed. The glass curtain wall, with its clumsy grilles along floors devoted to mechanical equipment, looks like a tinny caricature of Corbu's majestic façades. The lobby of the Secretariat, with its black-and-white marble square and great lighting boxes, looks like a giant bathroom. The stairs and ramps – those sculptural counterpoints Corbu has always turned into such lovely flights of poetry – are hardly more sensitive in design than those leading into Gimbel's basement. And the office spaces in the Secretariat are so undistinguished that their best feature, in all likelihood, is that nobody seems to have designed them at all – a blessing when one considers some of the 'creative design' that has been employed to 'jazz up' several of the more public spaces in the Headquarters.

The General Assembly building turned out to be a particular offender, and for a rather amusing reason. The scheme finally accepted by the Board of Design had *two* pie-shaped auditorium spaces in the General Assembly structure, placed back to back so that the over-all shape of the plan resembled a sort of hourglass, with the entrance at the narrow waist, and the two assembly halls spreading out from the central entrance lobby. As the working drawings were further developed, the UN decided to cut out one of the two assembly halls for reasons of economy. This would, normally, have forced a major change in the over-all shape of the General Assembly building, and thus involved a recall of the Board of Design (including Corbu) to reconsider that aspect of the plan. By this time Harrison was thoroughly fed up with Corbu's histrionics; the thought of having to cope with him again was too much to bear. So he went to work, with the help of several bright young designers, to try to retain the exterior hourglass shape of the plan, but fill it with only one assembly hall instead of two. This project proved to be about as easy as trying to fit a mermaid into a pair of pants, and about as successful. When the building was finally completed in 1952, the *Architectural Forum* hailed it as a departure from form-follows-function and 'some loosening of surrounding dogma'. That was perhaps the understatement of the year in architectural circles. Dogma was not the only thing that had to be loosened to get a single auditorium to fit a double-auditorium shell. Paul Rudolph, the young architect who was later to head the School of Architecture at Yale, was considerably more penetrating in his brash comments.

The interiors of the UN Assembly Building [he informed the readers of the *Architectural Forum*] bring the so-called International Style close to bankruptcy. Of course the building is not really a product of the International Style but rather a background for a Grade 'B' movie about 'One World' with Rita Hayworth dancing up the main ramp. . . . Le Corbusier's diagram unfortunately did not indicate the way for the interiors of the UN Assembly Building.

And Serge Chermayeff, one of the most articulate of the early members of CIAM, summed it all up by saying that 'the geometry and texture of Le Corbusier's sketch are there and make their point, but the "executed" detail and the concept do not jell . . .'

Still, to most people, the UN Headquarters probably represents an impressive statement of the power of which modern architecture is capable. If so, this effect is due primarily to the sketch proposal made by Corbu (and the years of work that preceded it) and, secondly, to the technically competent execution of the sketch by Harrison. For the building does show a neat competence that few European architects were then able to equal: nothing has leaked (except for the windows, which were put to an unexpected test one day when it started to rain *upward*! The reason was that the glass façades created a violent updraft of warm air just outside the building, and this updraft carried gusts of rain with it. The windows were subsequently fixed to cope with both down- and up-pours); the elevators and the air-conditioning work beautifully (which is more than can be said about certain European buildings); and life and work, in general, are pleasant in the gleaming Headquarters. Only by comparison with Corbu's executed work of the postwar years does the UN seem a failure in many of its details.

While Corbu appeared increasingly bitter and cantankerous during these years – to the outside world, at least – he remained, in the private reality of a few close friendships, a charming and warm person. One of his friends in New York was the sculptor Tino Nivola. Born in Sardinia of a peasant family, Nivola has the sort of primitive and uncomplicated charm that Corbu always felt he could trust. While the UN battles were being fought uptown during the day, Corbu spent many evenings and week-ends in Nivola's 8th Street studio, in Greenwich Village, painting his passionate, brightly coloured canvases. In later years, when Corbu had come to the conclusion that almost everyone in America was a potential enemy, Nivola seemed to be one of the few exceptions. On his occasional visits to the U.S., Corbu liked to go out to Amaganssett, at the end of Long Island, where Nivola has an old-fashioned frame-and-clapboard house; and there the great man, dressed only in shorts, a sports shirt, and the inevitable black-rimmed glasses, would make sand sculptures on the beach, using a poured-plaster process developed by his friend, or play with Nivola's children in the garden behind the house. On one such week-end Corbu decided to repay his host for his generous and uncomplicated hospitality: he did it by painting two huge murals on adjoining plaster walls inside the little clapboard house. In this setting, among children, trees, the ocean, and simple and friendly people, Corbu relaxed and showed himself to be a warm and kindly human being. Oddly enough, it was the city, which he loved so much, that produced most of his real or imagined enemies. 'I first really began to understand Corbu when I met his wife,' Nivola said. 'She was a wonderful and funny, primitive type, the only person who never really took Corbu very seriously as a great figure.' Le Corbusier must have found some of the same qualities in Nivola and in other close friends. These were the people he felt he could trust – not the sophisticates who were attracted by Corbu's own enormous sophistication.

Corbu's reputation as an *enfant terrible*, incapable of collaboration with others on an equal basis, cost him at least one other important commission that might have been his. Shortly after the UN Headquarters was completed in New York, UNESCO decided that it must have a Headquarters of its own, separate from the parent organization in Manhattan. Paris was the natural seat for UNESCO; and it appeared obvious that in Paris, at least, there could be no argument against having Corbu design the buildings. Just as an administrative centre on the skyscraper-studded island of Manhattan seemed to call for a man just like Harrison, who knew skyscraper organization better than just about anyone else of his generation, so a cultural centre in Paris called for the one architect who represented with the greatest distinction the traditions of modern French culture. Yet, as a large part of the money for the UNESCO Headquarters was provided by the United States, officials of the State Department had a major say in the selection of UNESCO's architect. They felt that diplomacy must be an essential quality in the architect to be selected, as the Paris authorities tended to be hostile to a modern structure – and, in particular, to any *tall* modern building. Corbu had not distinguished himself particularly in his political dealings with French authorities any more than he had in his dealings with some American officials; and while this was due as much to the stupidity and narrowness of officialdom in Paris as it was to Corbu's aggressiveness, it represented an existing, political fact of life and had to be considered.

To make sure that Corbu would not get the UNESCO job, the UNESCO people and the State Department men most directly concerned decided to set up a board whose job it would be to select the architects for UNESCO, and then made Corbu a member of that board. Everyone concerned realized that this was a device to take Corbu out of the running, as the board could hardly select one of its own members. As a matter of fact, the board did select three excellent men: Marcel Breuer, the Hungarian-born American architect who is probably the closest counterpart to Corbu in the U.S.; Pier Luigi Nervi, the brilliant Italian engineer whose speciality is precast, reinforced concrete and who could teach Corbu and others a thing or two about the technical problems involved in handling this material; and Bernard Zehrfuss, a young French architect of tact and good political connexions. This team completed its job in 1958, when the UNESCO Headquarters on the place de Fontenoy were opened to the general public. The achievement was considerable; and though it owed much to Corbu in its details, it reflected many original contributions that had been arrived at independently of Le Corbusier. Throughout the planning stage of UNESCO, Corbu tried, by all sorts of means, to get his hand in. It was tragic to see how bitterly hurt he was to have been denied this third (and possibly final) opportunity to realize his League of Nations Palace.

There is really nothing reprehensible in Corbu's inability to work harmoniously with others. Art-by-committee is a ridiculous notion; even Walter Gropius, who greatly favours collaboration among technicians to solve today's architectural and planning problems, does not really believe that a great work of art can emerge from such collaboration unless a great architect dominates the collaborative effort. (The UNESCO job was largely dominated by Breuer.) Yet the world of organization men is constantly on the lookout for other, safe organization men to whom it can entrust its problems; and the result – most clearly visible in the postwar buildings in Manhattan – is a mess of mediocrity. The criticism so often levelled against Corbu that he is 'unreasonable' is no criticism at all; if Corbu had been 'reasonable', he would never have succeeded in doing what he did. 'When we began our symphony,' Corbu once said, 'our continual role was to appear as tough guys, with dirty, muddy boots stamping into an elegant and tranquil society in order to assert our ways of thinking. And so it happened that our attitude was insolent, despite ourselves . . .' The tragedy of Corbu's life has been not that he has grown bitter, but that he knew, almost from the start, that the price he had to pay for achieving his objectives was to live a life of bitterness. And the greatness of Corbu's life is his indestructible optimism in spite of that bitterness.

When he completed the Marseille block in 1952, Corbu demonstrated several obvious things: first, he showed (at long last) what he meant by his vertical city of gardens and piazzas in the sky. Second, he showed that he was capable, at an age that would lead most architects to thoughts of retirement, to start out on an entirely new and brilliant career as a plastic artist – a career so dazzling as to leave his many younger followers once again far behind. But he showed something else, far less obvious: he showed he knew that the role of an artist cannot be to try to gain popular acceptance, but that artists must be willing to challenge popularly accepted men and ideas with creative, individual statements of a strength that no one could ignore.

In a sense Marseille liberated Corbu from his fruitless struggles of three or four decades to try to become an accepted, 'well-integrated' member of society. From now on, Corbu seems to have felt, he was not going to deal with political situations; now his work would be a statement of what he thought, not as a frequently rejected member of polite society, but as a creative artist, standing alone.

The buildings constructed by Corbu from 1950 on have a plastic inventiveness and grandeur comparable to some of the most powerful monuments produced by man since the beginnings of recorded history. Each of the great structures completed by him during those years seemed to be another brilliant sculptural achievement. From the massively formed chapel at Ronchamp [40] in the Vosges Mountains, all the way to the government buildings at Chandigarh, the new capital of the Punjab, Corbu – once the man of the cube and the cylinder – brought back into architecture a magic world of

40. Ronchamp. (Photo: Lucien Hervé)

41. *The interior of the chapel at Ronchamp. The deep slots in the wall are filled with brightly coloured glass.* (*Photo: Lucien Hervé*)

plastic form and virile texture which had been notably missing in the work of all modernists except, perhaps, in that of Frank Lloyd Wright. Yet, where Wright's plasticity was often indistinguishable from the nature forms of the Art Nouveau (and, hence, dated), Corbu's new world of form seems to be timeless, conceivably the product of any and all ages, modern in every respect and ancient in

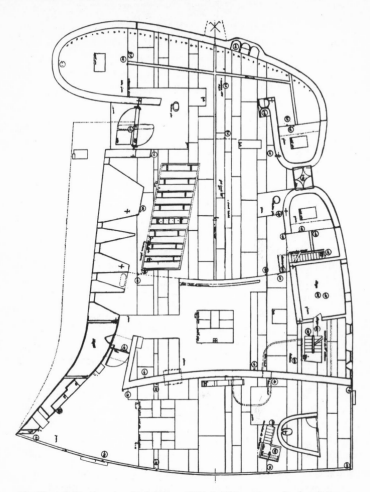

42. Plan of the chapel at Ronchamp, 1950–3. This pure work of sculpture is based, according to Le Corbusier, upon the proportionate scale of the Modulor. (From Œuvre complète)

every respect also. The great curved masses of Ronchamp might be the result of some acoustic determination, as Corbu declared; but they formed, together with the deep, irregularly spaced slot windows in the walls, a mysterious aura that was as reminiscent of the cata-combs or the massive stone monasteries of the Middle Ages as it was of some dimly understood spatial concepts of today and tomorrow. 'An implacable mathematics and physics reign over the forms presented to the eye,' Corbu said. 'Their agreement, their repetition, their interdependence, and the spirit of unity or of family which binds them together to form an architectural expression, is a phenomenon which is as supple, subtle, exact and implacable as that of acoustics.' It is characteristic of Le Corbusier that even in as individual a sculptural statement as Ronchamp he tried to express and experiment with certain mathematical rules that would have broader application to the world at large. To Corbu, the idea of an art without a body of laws is totally irresponsible. Once, in Long Island, when he saw the late Jackson Pollock's 'automatic' paintings, he said that he thought that painting, to be valid, must admit to certain fundamental rules. So even this sprayed-concrete sculpture on a hill above the river Saône was an attempt to dramatize the rule of law in all life and in all art. To a Frenchman, there is nothing stultifying about a rule of law, as there was to an American radical like Wright. The rule of law is a poetic vision; and Corbu actually wrote and published a 'Poem to the Right Angle' in the years when Ronchamp was being designed!

Throughout his life Corbu has searched for a rule of law in art. The idea that this made him a functionalist appalled and repelled him. 'This frightful word was born under other skies than those I have always loved – those where the sun reigns supreme,' he said, with a characteristic slap at the U.S., whose Horatio Greenough is generally credited with inventing the term 'functionalism'. Corbu's concept of a rule of law is intimately tied to a rule of life; and his Modulor system is a beautiful expression of what he means.

The Modulor is not a system of repetitive, identical dimensions of the dreary sort familiar to quantity surveyors and such, but rather a system of related proportions based upon the ancient 'Golden Section' and the human figure that reflects that Section. In general, the Modulor starts with the division of the height of a man into two proportions, at the waistline. These two proportions, according to Corbu, govern all other dimensions of the human body: for example, a man with his arm naturally upraised creates another Modulor proportion, the distance between his head and his waist being in the proper relation to the distance between his head and his fingertips. Starting with this interlocking system of proportions – fingertips to head to waistline to soles of feet – Corbu developed a gradually diminishing scale of proportionate dimensions. In Corbu's studio at 35 rue de Sèvres each draughtsman and designer has a list of related Modulor dimensions pinned up on the wall next to his or her drawing-board. The list consists of only two columns of ten numbers each. According to Le Corbusier this proportionate scale (applicable to the design of anything from a piazza to a bookshelf) has one further advantage: it is apparently the only numerical scale that relates the foot-and-inch system to the metric system, and vice versa.

It is characteristic of Corbu that a good deal of mysticism and poetic passion have surrounded the Modulor system. For while this is a real attempt to introduce a rule of law, related to both nature and art, into an industrial architecture, the project in Corbu's mind has nothing to do with the adding machine. It represents to him a

43. Modulor figure by Le Corbusier, showing developments of proportionate system based on divisions of the human figure. Lowest permissible ceiling height is that of man with upraised arm. (From Œuvre complète)

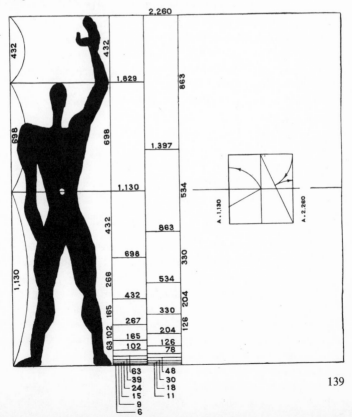

system of ultimate truths; and, like all ultimate truths, the Modulor figures did not mean much until he was able to reduce them to an extremely precise code. To anyone but a Frenchman this sort of thing might seem pedantic in the extreme; indeed, anyone but a Frenchman would probably be incapable of achieving a Modulor system. Not long ago Corbu became convinced that some 'American gangsters' were trying to steal his Modulor by setting up a company called something like Modular Structures. Not only was he being silly, but he missed the most important point about his own invention: every modular system developed in the U.S. and elsewhere is a system based upon a single dimension, repeated and multiplied *ad infinitum*. (The most commonly used dimensions in the U.S. range from four inches to four feet, with multiples of four inches occasionally employed for certain prefabricated units.) But such systems are, of course, simple-minded by comparison with Corbu's Modulor, which does not use a single dimensional module, but only an infinite series of *related dimensions*. When Corbu showed the Modulor to the late Albert Einstein, in Princeton, Einstein told him that this was 'a range of dimensions which makes the bad difficult and the good easy'. This moral and poetic basis of the Modulor inspired Corbu to make the system, in a sense, the culmination of a life's work devoted to bringing a rule of law into art. Many critics, who admire Corbu's individual buildings, have scoffed at his various odes to the Modulor, not realizing that to this intensely moral man it was essential to develop a system that would 'make the bad difficult and the good easy', to hand on to generations to come. It is an essential part of Corbu's greatness that he has *never* produced a single work that did not, in some way, contribute to the solution of a broader problem in architecture and city planning. The critics might admire the masses and spaces of the Marseille block – and rightly so; but, to Corbu, one of the most important aspects of the Marseille building is the fact that it is dimensioned completely according to the Modulor system of proportions. At the entrance to the building, cast in a slab of concrete, there stands Corbu's Modulor figure of a man with upraised arm [44]; near by, there is a concrete block on which the Modulor proportions used in this building are precisely incised. 'It is in such moments as these,' Corbu said, 'that architecture soars, leaving the brutal and the material and attaining to spirituality.' The rule of law by which civilized men live is the single, most moving political and moral

44. Relief in concrete by Le Corbusier, based upon his Modulor Figure. These figures can be found at the base of every apartment building by Le Corbusier. This one is from the apartments at Berlin, completed in 1958. (Photo: Peter Blake)

achievement of the West. The rule of law which Corbu has tried to bring into architecture may, someday, be considered the single most moving contribution he has made to our culture.

Although Ronchamp was almost pure sculpture, this chapel, too – according to Le Corbusier – was developed according to this moral code. But the use of the Modulor is much more evident in Corbu's several other apartment blocks built after Marseille – the block at Nantes, the similar block in West Berlin (sadly defaced by Corbu's insensitive German clients), the new Brazilian Pavilion in the University City in Paris [45], the beautiful Secretariat Building at Chandigarh [46] (which, incidentally, shows what a Corbu-designed UN Secretariat might have been like), and in several other structures done both in Asia and in Europe during the late 1950s.

45. Detail of the Brazilian Pavilion, University City, Paris, 1957–9. This building by Le Corbusier and Lucio Costa shows a highly refined use of 'brute concrete' contrasted with handsomely precast surfaces. (Photo: Peter Blake)

Each of these is a more extraordinary revelation of Corbu's mastery of brute forms than the one preceding it, each a more convincing proof of the importance of Corbu's 'reincarnation' after the Second World War.

In these monumental and virile structures Le Corbusier has come to physical grips with the material he loves, the material he recognizes to be the most exciting structural development in our time: reinforced concrete, now become 'reconstructed stone'. Lewis Mumford, who once called Corbu's brutal use of concrete 'sloppy', entirely missed the point: for Corbu is not only trying to leave the imprint of man on an architecture of the machine age – the imprint of man's hands in the rough form work, and the imprint of man's scale through the Modulor. He is also saying that the people of the earth must face the fact that the sort of architectural slickness

46. Detail of the façade of the Secretariat at Chandigarh. Although the pattern of balconies and sun-control louvres seems quite irregular, it adheres strictly to the proportionate scale of the Modulor. (Photo: Vernon Gibberd)

practised nowadays in the U.S. becomes more and more unrealistic as our natural and industrial resources fail to keep up with the incredible growth in the earth's population. *Le béton brut* is not only an aesthetic choice; it is the rational choice of the three to four billion population of the globe. It is the universal material, infinitely flexible, almost infinitely available, and capable of receiving the imprint of man's hand.

TWENTY

Shortly after Le Corbusier turned seventy, in the autumn of 1957, his wife died. Few people knew how severe a blow this was to him. A few years earlier he had been in Berlin to open an exhibition of his work, and he seemed tired and not in the best of health. Things were not going as well as they might: in Berlin the builders of his Marseille-type apartment block had ignored his drawings and changed the carefully designed fenestration into deadly bands of ribbon windows. Corbu's blasts at this and other examples of barbarism were, as usual, on the front pages of all local newspapers. But he did not seem to relish the battle as much as he once had. There were flashes of his old dynamism, though, when – during the opening of his exhibition – crowds of young men and women jostled to get his signature on copies of his books, tried to shake his hand, applauded whenever he appeared. Even in the alleged capital of youthful nihilism, Corbu could stir young people almost as if he were a famous jazz or film star . . . He obviously enjoyed himself in those moments: and the crooked, slightly sarcastic smile on his thin face made him look very much younger than his seventy years.

Though his wife was dead, and he had broken with his collaborator of the postwar years, the young Yugoslav, Wogensky, Corbu was fortunate in at least one respect: like Mies van der Rohe and others of their generation, Corbu was busier than ever before. Much of his work was at Chandigarh, the new capital of the Punjab, the city Corbu had been able to plan from scratch and whose centre was being designed entirely by him [47]. Chandigarh, until a few years ago merely a windswept plain at the foot of the Himalayas, was rising as the first city born entirely out of Corbu's genius.

Most of the work at Chandigarh had to be housing, of course; and for that part of the job Corbu brought in two English members of CIAM, Maxwell Fry and his wife, Jane Drew; and he also asked his cousin, Pierre Jeanneret, with whom he had been in partnership until the German invasion of France broke up their office, to come

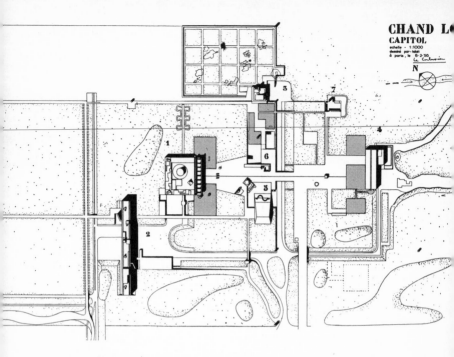

CHAND L(
CAPITOL
echelle - 1:1000
dessiné par-talab
à paris, le 8-2-56
Le Corbusier
N

47. Plan of the Capitol at Chandigarh, 1950–7. (1) is the Parliament Building or Assembly Hall; (2) is the Secretariat; (3) is the Governor's Palace; (4) is the Palace of Justice; and (7) is the 'Monument of the Open Hand'. (From Œuvre complète)

and help design the housing units. But the core of Chandigarh, the heart of this city, Corbu reserved for himself. This, he seemed to feel, was going to be the culmination of everything that went before.

And so it is. Words are not quite adequate to describe the power of Chandigarh. Its centre is in the tradition of Corbu's project for Saint-Dié, though the elements that make up the great plaza are all governmental: a square Assembly building, the parliament; an 800-foot-long Secretariat, eight storeys high; a small, square Governor's Palace; the Palace of Justice; and several related elements of landscaping on different levels. Finally, there is the 'Monument of the Open Hand', off to one side of the great plaza.

The first building to be completed was the Palace of Justice [48, 49, and 50], a fantastic, vaulted structure topped by a huge, concrete roof umbrella that shelters a four-storey, wall-less entrance lobby

48. Principal façade of the Palace of Justice. A huge parasol of concrete cools and shades the building proper. The concrete vaults are irregular, but fit into the Modulor scale. (Photo: Vernon Gibberd)

lined with concrete ramps and topped by arches. To both sides of this great lobby are courtrooms on several levels, protected by an irregular concrete grille of sun breakers. Corbu's bright pastel colours – vermilion, pastel blue, lemon yellow, white – are used as accents behind the concrete grille and contrast brilliantly with the *béton brut* of the structure. Here the concrete, in all its unfinished roughness, has emerged looking as wonderfully coarse as a rock formation moulded by thousands of years of wind and rain. Here, better than at Marseille, Corbu achieved the timelessness that will make his architecture a permanent treasure of man's history.

In the great courtrooms the necessary sound absorbent surfaces are provided by huge tapestries designed by Corbu himself. Below the parasol roof, there are terraces and penthouses that overlook the plaza below and the city beyond – all the way to the foothills of the Himalayas. Wherever you look, this building offers new and unexpected spatial experiences – streaks of sunlight cutting through an opening in the structure, unexpectedly lighting up an interior concrete wall; ramps, balconies, arches, columns, a patch of the sky. Curiously enough, most of Corbu's achievements up to that time had been in the general area of form and exterior space. Here, in the Palace of Justice, Corbu showed himself a master of *interior* space as well.

147

49. *Interior of the Palace of Justice, Chandigarh, 1953. Flying ramps connect the various levels of the building. (Photo: Lucien Hervé)*

The lovely scale models of Chandigarh, made for Corbu by turbaned and heavily bearded Indian model makers, were carved out of solid blocks of walnut (or its Indian equivalent). In a sense, this abstraction of architectural forms through the use of a *natural* material (instead of plastic, say) is very revealing of Corbu's *rapprochement* to nature. It would have been inconceivable for him to make the models of the great 'pure prisms' of the 1920s of anything but metal, plastics, and glass.

The Secretariat was completed next. It is a building rather similar in character to the Marseille block, though much more assured in its finish. Here, too, Corbu was able to show his fellow architects a few things they might study with profit: for example, while many U.S. architects think little of covering an 800-foot-long façade with a repetitive pattern of *identical* 'curtain-wall' units, it was quite

50. *Concrete pyramids set into a circular splash-basin at the foot of the Palace of Justice. (Photo: Vernon Gibberd)*

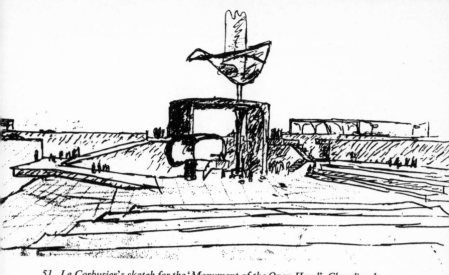

51. Le Corbusier's sketch for the 'Monument of the Open Hand', Chandigarh. The great metal hand will turn in the wind like a weathervane. The building sketched at the right is the Palace of Justice. (From Œuvre complète)

obvious to Corbu that such treatment could lead only to endless monotony. The 800-foot-long façades of the Secretariat are broken in half a dozen places with projections, recesses, stair towers, changes in pattern, and the like. All these contrasting elements – like everything else at Chandigarh – are related to one another through the proportionate scale of the Modulor, so that all things have a family resemblance and general harmony. But apart from this over-all harmony, contrast is everpresent – contrast again as an expression of the selective, human act.

The third completed building at Chandigarh is the Assembly Hall, a wonderful play of concrete cubes against gigantic free-form elements, also of concrete. This building must be compared with the U.S. Capitol in Washington – a symmetrical structure symbolizing an asymmetrical process: for in Washington the Senate chamber is 'expressed' in precisely the same way as that of the House of Representatives, despite the fact that the first contains fewer than a fourth of the members of the second, and despite the fact that the two vary radically in influence.

This curious relationship between Upper and Lower Houses has been beautifully expressed in Corbu's Assembly Hall at Chandigarh. The first is a small, four-sided pyramidal prism; the second is a huge,

hyperbolic-paraboloid form, similar in shape to the thin-shell concrete cooling towers familiar to industry. These two symbolic forms
are placed inside a large 'forum' which, in turn, is surrounded on its
four sides by galleries containing offices and committee meeting
rooms. The two symbolic forms are not swallowed up by this mass of
surrounding offices, however; they are permitted to penetrate the
roof and thus to reach for the sky – both poetically and literally, for
most of their interior light is derived from skylights on top. A massive,
three-storey-high portico forms a monumental entrance that faces
the Palace of Justice a quarter of a mile away. The Assembly Hall
was dedicated in 1961.

The two most important remaining structures are yet to be built:
they are the Governor's Palace, symbolizing the executive branch of
the government, and the 'Monument of the Open Hand' [51].

This monument is a marvellous fantasy, reminiscent of Corbu's
proposed memorial to Vaillant-Couturier, done right after the
end of the Second World War. It is a fifty-foot-high structure of
wood, covered with hammered iron in a process that is in common
use in the Punjab, and set on a huge ball-bearing so that the great
upraised hand might turn in the wind like a weathervane 'to indicate,
symbolically, the state of affairs . . .' Regardless of the validity (or
presence) of any symbolism of government, this is really Corbu's
personal symbol of man *vis-à-vis* nature – the white, upraised cube,
held against the sky; the upraised Acropolis, silhouetted against the
sky; the upraised hand of the Modulor figure – a kind of Atlas
figure supporting man's noblest creation, architecture, and offering
it up to the sun.

Chandigarh was only a part of Corbu's work in the late 1950s.
At Ahmedabad, the centre of India's cotton-spinning area, he had
completed his first museum, much along the lines proposed by him
twenty years earlier. At Ahmedabad, also, he had built several
beautiful houses of *béton brut*, as strong as some medieval monastic
structures; and a building for the mill owners' association, with an
assembly hall of sweeping, curved forms. There was more work in
Asia, the Middle East, and Europe – another museum, this one in
Japan; the landscaping for a dam in India; houses, exhibitions
(including the extraordinary sculptural pavilion at the Brussels
World's Fair for the Phillips Industries – a structure of precast-
concrete units forming a series of interlocking hyperbolic para-
boloids). And, at long last, there was a commission in the United

States as well – to build a new Arts Center for Harvard University. Whatever Corbu planned and built, he tried to make speak in a universal language, applicable to all mankind, understandable in terms of both the past and the present, and prophetic of the future.

Many years earlier, in *Vers une architecture*, the young Le Corbusier had written this about two men – Michelangelo and Phidias:

Intelligence and passion; there is no art without emotion, no emotion without passion. Stones are dead things sleeping in the quarries, but the apses of St Peter's are a drama. The drama of architecture is that of the man who lives by and through the universe. As the man, so the drama, so the architecture. We must not assert . . . that the masses give rise to their man. A *man* is an exceptional phenomenon, occurring at long intervals, perhaps by chance . . .

Michelangelo is the man of the last thousand years, just as Phidias was the man of the thousand years before. The work of Michelangelo is a *creation*, not a Renaissance . . . A passion, an intelligence beyond normal – this was the Everlasting Yea.

Phidias, the great sculptor who made the Parthenon. There has been nothing like it anywhere or at any period . . . For two thousand years, those who have seen the Parthenon have felt that here was a decisive moment in architecture.

We are now at such a decisive moment.

Phidias, Michelangelo, Le Corbusier. Intelligence and Passion; the Everlasting Yea; the Decisive Moment.

The books about Le Corbusier are unusually numerous – few modern architects are so well documented – and the great bulk of them fall into two classes: detailed publication of his buildings, and writings by Le Corbusier himself.

In the first category the outstanding work is *Le Corbusier: Œuvre complète,* vols. I-IV, edited by Willy Boesiger and published by Ginsberger of Zürich (distributed by George Wittenborn Inc., New York). This is the ultimate source of information about all his published buildings. Since it has now become very cumbersome, an abridged edition, by the same editor and publisher, has been brought out in one volume under the title of *Le Corbusier: 1910-1960.*

One single building of great importance is covered in *The Marseilles Block* by Le Corbusier, translated by Geoffrey Sainsbury and published by the Harvill Press, London.

General and theoretical works by Le Corbusier include the following, of which the first two are of outstanding importance: *Towards a New Architecture,* the classic of 1923 translated by Frederick Etchells (Frederick A. Praeger Inc., New York), and *The City of Tomorrow* (Harcourt, Brace & World Inc., New York), a town-planning companion to the previous title, also translated by Etchells. More recent are *The Home of Man* (Architectural Press, London) and *Concerning Town Planning* (Yale University Press, New Haven, Conn.), and there is also a highly personal essay on *The Chapel at Ronchamp* (Frederick A. Praeger Inc.). One recent work of consequence is *The Four Routes,* and this is published by Dobson, London.

Le Corbusier's own explanation of his famous dimensional system will be found in *Modulor I* and *Modulor II,* both published by Harvard University Press, Cambridge, Mass.

Books about Le Corbusier by other hands are few and not very accessible, though the compact and recent (if one-sided) *Le Corbusier* by Françoise Choay deserves to be mentioned; it is published by George Braziller Inc., New York, in the Masters of World Architecture series, and is also available in paperback from Pocket Books, New York. Some criticism and explanation of Le Corbusier's early writings will be found in the relevant chapters of *Theory and Design in the*

First Machine Age by Reyner Banham, published by Frederick A. Praeger Inc.

Finally, one may mention three magazine articles, which should be accessible through any good library that subscribes to the *Architectural Review:* 'The Mathematics of the Ideal Villa,' by Colin Rowe, March 1947; 'The Space Machine,' by Lionel Brett, November 1947; and 'Garches to Jaoul,' by James Stirling, September 1955.

INDEX

Italic numbers refer to illustrations